Constructing White-Collar Crime

University of Pennsylvania Press
Law in Social Context Series

A complete list of the books in this series
appears at the back of this volume.

Constructing
White-Collar Crime

Rationalities,
Communication, Power

Joachim J. Savelsberg

with contributions by
Peter Brühl

University of Pennsylvania Press

Philadelphia

This volume is based on Joachim J. Savelsberg and Peter Brühl, *Politik und Wirtschaftsstrafrecht: Rationalitäten, Kommunikationen und Macht* (Opladen: Leske & Budrich, 1988), revised, translated, and with a new chapter on the United States.

Library of Congress Cataloging-in-Publication Data
Savelsberg, Joachim J., 1951–
    Constructing white-collar crime : rationalities, communication, power /
Joachim J. Savelsberg ; with contributions by Peter Brühl.
        p.   cm. — (Law in social context series)
    "Based on Joachim J. Savelsberg and Peter Brühl, Politik und Wirtschaftsstrafrecht:
rationalitäten, kommunikationen und macht (Opladen: Leske & Budrich, 1988),
revised, translated, and with a new chapter on the United States"—Copyright page.
    Includes bibliographical references and index.
    ISBN 0-8122-3240-2
    1. Commercial crimes—Germany (West)—Political aspects.   2. White collar
crimes—Germany (West)—Political aspects.   3. Legislation—Germany (West)
4. Commercial crimes—United States—Political aspects.   5. White collar crimes—
United States—Political aspects.   6. Legislation—United States.   I. Brühl, Peter.
II. Savelsberg, Joachim J., 1951–   Politik und Wirtschaftsstrafrecht.   III. Title.
IV. Series.
KK6864.S275   1994
345.73′0268—dc20
[347.305268]   93-46048
                                                                                              CIP

Contents

Figures and Tables

Preface

> The ambiguous nature of white-collar crimes . . . is exactly what makes them so interesting from a sociological point of view and what gives us a clue to important norm conflicts, clashing group interests, and maybe incipient social change . . . The major variables which account for the defining of such acts as crimes seem to be connected with the concept of multiple social hierarchies or diverse status systems.
> Vilhelm Aubert, "White-Collar Crime and Social Structure" (1952, pp. 266, 271)

For most Western countries, including the United States of America (US) and the Federal Republic of Germany (FRG), the 1960s and 1970s witnessed an international trend to criminalize the deviance of white-collar offenders. For example, in 1976 and 1986 the German legislature passed long-debated bills against economic crime, criminalizing offenses such as subsidy- and credit-related fraud, offenses tied to bankruptcy and usury, computer crimes, and credit card fraud. Both pieces of legislation were preceded by a first-ever debate on economic crime at the 49th meeting of the German Lawyers Association (*Deutscher Juristentag*) in 1972. They were prepared by the 1972–78 work of a Commission for the Fight Against Economic Crime, established by the Federal Department of Justice. These activities in the political sector, the legal profession, and by criminologists were embedded in a social climate and movement that became increasingly mistrustful of powerful economic actors. As reported in the important news media analyzed for this study, the number of critical claims against economic offenders tripled between the early 1960s and the early 1970s and then stabilized. The proportion of citizens who believe that entrepreneurs engage in dirty deals and lack conscience increased from 10 percent in 1965 to 25 percent in 1983. Yet attempts to criminalize some types of severe entrepreneurial deviance, for example antitrust offenses and especially bid rigging, failed despite this general climate and a forceful social movement.

This book presents a socio-legal analysis of the legislation against economic offenses in the federal government of the FRG. We concentrate on the 1986 Second Law Against Economic Crime and the societal context of this legislation. We find that the German case against economic deviance provides commonalities with the American experience as well as divergences from it. Throughout this book we make references to American cases, the concluding chapter explicitly discusses the American situation and draws comparative conclusions.

We use the term "white-collar crime" despite its lack of precision. The term refers to economic and political crimes, organizational and occupational offenses, and non-work-related crimes of high status individuals. We use this general term because it is used in society. It carries symbolic meaning, has political implications, and thus constitutes social reality. We will see that the meaning of the term shifts in the course of the legislative process. While those who introduced the term aimed primarily at powerful corporate offenders, the legislative outcome criminalizes primarily the lower echelons of the white-collar hierarchy, computer programmers, for example. It is exactly the flexibility of the term that makes it a useful instrument in the political process.

Our approach is sociological. We recognize that criminal laws are social facts, constructed in political processes. Everyday theories about crime as well as criminological writings frequently disregard this fact. Most debates on the political construction of criminal law continue to lack theoretically guided empirical insights on the quality of these political processes, on the decisions they result in, and on the rationales and social forces guiding these decisions. These debates also lack an internationally comparative perspective.

This book works on all of these fronts. It presents an empirical case study, it includes internationally comparative analysis, and the empirical investigation is theoretically guided. We want to use the data to learn about the relative validity of competing theoretical traditions in the sociology of criminal law. We take two overlapping controversies into special consideration, one between Marxist and pluralist approaches, the other between functionalist and conflict group or action theory approaches. Max Weber's classical thoughts about the substantive rationalization of law, that is, the intrusion of ethical, economic, and sociological reasoning on the formal rational quality of law, proves to be a fruitful guide when we try to understand the development of recent economic crime legislation.

Finally, this research is methodologically innovative. It introduces the cognitive mapping approach into the study of criminal justice legislation. We found this approach most helpful in trying to understand the reasoning of decision makers, in discovering consistencies and inconsistencies between arguments presented by different actors, or by a particular actor in different situations, on different types of offenses, offenders, and victims. We relate these patterns of argumentation to the structural, organizational, and societal conditions to which decision makers are exposed. We thus bridge the gap between micro- and macro-sociological approaches to the construction of criminal law.

The interdisciplinary collaboration of Joachim J. Savelsberg, a sociologist, and Peter Brühl, a lawyer, proved essential for the realization of this project. While Brühl's legal expertise was crucial throughout the project, he also wrote the sections on the lobbying of industrial organizations, based on research in the archives of the most powerful German Industry Federation (*Bund der Deutschen Industrie*). Most of the text was written by Savelsberg. Sections authored by Brühl are specifically identified.

We are indebted to several institutions and persons who have provided time and resources. Research on comparative perspectives was promoted by Savelsberg's 1987–88 John F. Kennedy Memorial Fellowship at Harvard University. Funding for two and a half years of research on the German case study was provided by the West German National Science Foundation (*Deutsche Forschungsgemeinschaft*, Project Number Ha 1014/10-1-3). The University of Bremen (Research Section on Social Problems) provided the institutional base for the realization of this project. Frequent intellectual exchange at Bremen, especially with Hans Haferkamp, Peter Boy, Johannes Feest, Volkmar Gessner, Wolfgang Jagodzinski, Hans-Günther Heiland, Rüdiger Lautmann, Christian Lüdemann, and Karl F. Schumann helped us tremendously.

Hans Haferkamp, then chair of the theory section of the German Sociological Association, inspired and helped to initiate the empirical project. It is not without consequences for this project that Hans was in the process of organizing a joint session of the American and German theory sections on "Social Structure and Culture" while we conducted this project (Haferkamp 1989). His early death in 1987 was a tragic loss for his friends and for the sociological enterprise.

Our research assistants, Martina Voigt and Susann Weber, and—for the analysis of news media—Angelika Schade, Karen Patscheck, and Corinna Ahlers did a tremendous job. The demanding content analysis could not have been done without their reliability and industriousness.

James F. Short (Washington State University) and Francis Cullen (University of Cincinnati) carefully read the entire manuscript for the University of Pennsylvania Press. Their comments very much contributed to improving the American version of this book. Helpful suggestions for particular aspects of this project were provided by Matthew Bonham (American University), Waltraud N. Gallhofer and Willem F. Saris (University of Amsterdam), Robin Stryker (University of Iowa), and Hubert Treiber (University of Hannover). Presentations of aspects of this research provided fruitful discussions and comments at the 1985 Meeting of the Research Council for the Sociology of Law, International Sociological Association; the 1988 Meetings of the Society for the Study of Social Problems and the American Sociological Association; the National Institute of Justice, U.S. Department of Justice; the Social Theory Seminar of the Center for European Studies, Harvard University; the criminal justice and sociology departments of Temple University; the John Jay College for Criminal Justice, City University of New York; the School for Social Ecology at the University of California at Irvine; and the sociology departments of the universities of Bremen and Minnesota.

We thank Leske & Budrich, our German publishers, who welcomed the publication of this revised and extended English version of the 1988 German publication. Parts of the chapter on the expert commission previously appeared in *Law and Policy* 10, 2–3 (1988):215–252; parts of the theory chapter and of the section on the Judicial Committee appeared in *Law and Society Review* 21, 4 (1987):529–561. We thank Basil Blackwell Publishers and the Law and Society Association respectively for their permission to reprint these texts.

We finally have to thank numerous informants: representatives of the German government, especially the *Bundestag* and the Federal Department of Justice, and expert consultants of the government and representatives of lobby organizations, especially the German industry. Many participated in extensive interviews and provided valuable documents. This project could not have been realized without their generosity.

Part I
Why Study White-Collar
Crime Legislation?

Chapter 1
Questions, Introduction to the Case, and Overview

Ever since the late 1960s social movements and public opinion have increasingly called for equal justice in criminal law, demanding that crimes committed by the powerful also be prosecuted and punished (Katz 1980; Cullen et al. 1987, esp. pp. 1–36). These movements have been followed by considerable legislative activity and the passing of provisions against economic, white-collar, and organizational crime. Both the movements and the legislative efforts bloomed in several Western countries during the 1970s and 1980s, including the United States and the Federal Republic of Germany. Yet the social-structural distribution of those who were sentenced to prison did not change considerably during this period. Within the group of white-collar offenders those of relatively low prestige were most likely to be punished. Representative John Conyers (Detroit), then Chair of the Subcommittee on Criminal Justice of the U.S. House of Representatives, observed in 1988:

I am . . . wondering about when is a tax case a white-collar crime. I have had so much trouble with the IRS, which has been sending people to break down doors of doctors working in inner city neighborhoods who didn't pay their tax bill. . . . [T]hey are the ones who get the padlock on the door. They get their car snatched. . . . [Y]ou don't do that with the big tax boys—you don't take a business building and take that away from anybody. (U.S. House of Representatives, Subcommittee on Criminal Justice 1988, p. 490)

What Conyers, the politician, describes for the enforcement of criminal law—admittedly with a measure of hyperbole—has previously been demonstrated in scholarly research on prosecution (Hagan and Parker 1985) and criminal defense (Mann 1985). Only the sentencing stage in post-Watergate America seems to provide exceptions to the rule (Hagan, Nagel, and Albonetti 1980; Weisburd et al. 1991, pp. 128ff; Wheeler, Weisburd, and Bode 1982). Yet federal judges still seem to develop a special set of common law standards for white-collar offenders even in this sensitive period of American history (Mann, Wheeler, and Sarat 1980). Furthermore, when data from non-metropolitan districts are analyzed even in the sentencing stage of post-Watergate America researchers find that especially powerful white-collar offenders receive preferential treatment (Benson and Walker 1988).

Criminal law and justice tend to favor powerful offenders. This phenomenon is universal (Black 1976). We argue that legislation favors the powerful as well. Social movements and public expectations for the creation of *more* criminal law (against the powerful) for the sake of *more* justice are likely to be disappointed. These forces may be able to initiate legislation and enforcement but not to control them. The outcome of these processes therefore may well be counterproductive, resulting in more imprisonment and more class bias, not more justice.

Our study of one of the major legislative initiatives against economic crime in the West German government revealed, for example:

1. Members of the *Bundestag* (the equivalent of the U.S. House of Representatives) Judicial Committee switched their typical pro- or anti-punitive arguments on criminal justice issues when offenses of entrepreneurs were debated. Social Democratic representatives, who normally argue in favor of rehabilitation and social reform, took punitive positions, while conservative representatives, who mostly favor punitive responses to crime, stressed structural conditions of crime and the need for structural reform.
2. Arguments of the conservative faction in the judicial committee of the *Bundestag* on the proposed criminalization of bid-rigging, the most prominent case in our study, were almost exclusively of economic nature. Legal policy and criminal justice considerations were neglected. Does economic rationale determine what is right and wrong, what is criminal versus legal behavior? Our results show that this is, under certain conditions, the case.
3. Lines of conflict, which in public debates separate political parties, were predominantly drawn between the legal and economic branches of government when the criminalization of entrepreneurial offenders was discussed.

We will try to make sense of these and other findings by relating them to Max Weber's "sociology of law" (see Weber 1978) and to theories of social differentiation and domination. The empirical case is the legislative struggle over the Second Law Against Economic Crime (*Zweites Gesetz zur Bekämpfung der Wirtschaftskriminalität*), which the West German parliament passed in 1986. We concentrate on the attempted criminalization of serious antitrust offenses, especially bid rigging, one of the most intensely debated issues of this legislative process. We contrast this case with other provisions that were enacted to control behavior such as computer offenses and investment and credit card fraud. Why do some kinds of behavior become criminalized and not others? This study contributes some answers to this question. We first give an overview of the legislative process and outline the structure of this book.

From Push to Pull: A Short History of the Legislative Process

After a long period of inaction, some West German states (*Länder*) started to fight economic crime in the late 1960s. Special units were created in the police and the prosecutorial system, and special court chambers were also established. In 1972 economic crime was the main topic of the criminal law section of the 49th Meeting of the West German Lawyers Association (*Deutscher Juristentag*; see Chapter 4). Also in 1972 the Federal Department of Justice established a commission to develop a platform for the fight against economic crime. The commission held fifteen week-long meetings between 1972 and 1978. These meetings resulted in a long list of provisions which the commission passed on to the Justice Department (see Figure 1). The commission's work was accompanied by an intense debate on economic crime in criminal jurisprudence. In 1974 a new statistical program for the measurement of economic crime was institutionalized (Berckhauer 1980; Liebl 1984). And on September 1, 1976, the First Law Against Economic Crime (*Erstes Gesetz zur Bekämpfung der Wirtschaftskriminalität*) passed the House (*Bundestag*). Its measures were mostly based on suggestions developed by the commission. Its most important components were the criminalization of subsidy- and credit-related fraud and offenses tied to bankruptcy and usury.

The Federal Department of Justice consulted extensively with the justice departments of the states before, in 1978, it presented to the cabinet its first proposal for the Second Law Against Economic Crime. This bill was also largely based on the commission's suggestions. It took four years before the cabinet passed this bill in a modified form. Only in 1982 did the administration submit it to the legislative branch, a process that begins in the state chamber (*Bundesrat*). The chief targets

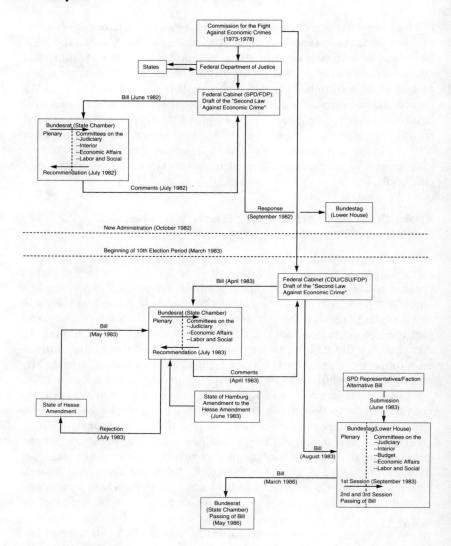

Figure 1. The legislative process.

of this proposal were computer-related fraud, forgery of computer data, fraud related to capital investment, and withdrawal of social security deductions by employers. The bill also reformed the criminal law provisions of the Stock Exchange Act (*Börsengesetz*) and clarified criminal liability in highly differentiated and complex organizations.

The extraordinarily long time it took for the first proposal of the Justice Department to be passed by the cabinet, and the modifications it underwent in this process, were due to the heavy involvement of industrial lobbying groups. These groups successfully worked toward the elimination of the proposed criminalization of antitrust offenses, especially bid rigging. The cabinet proposal passed the *Bundesrat* after a debate in plenary sessions and work in the committees for judicial, domestic, economic, and labor affairs. The *Bundesrat* then returned the bill including its own comments to the cabinet. The cabinet added a response and turned the whole package (bill and comments) over to the *Bundestag*.

After the 1982 change from the government coalition made up by the center-left Social Democratic Party (*Sozialdemokratische Partei Deutschlands*, SPD) and the small libertarian Free Democratic Party (*Freie Demokratische Partei*, FDP) to a coalition composed of the FDP and the conservative Christian Democratic Union/Christian Social Union (*Christlich-Demokratische Union/Christlich-Soziale Union*, CDU/CSU), the latter coalition reintroduced the proposal to the parliamentary process. The Social Democrats, now in the opposition and freed from their former libertarian coalition partner, reintroduced the bid rigging provision in the state chamber through two SPD-controlled states, Hesse and Hamburg. This and one later attempt in the House also failed. Again, the state chamber passed the bill and its comments back to the cabinet which sent the whole package to the House. The administration and an alternative bill presented by a group of social democratic representatives were under legislative debate in several committees of the *Bundestag* for more than two years. Unusual delays prevented the passing of the cabinet proposal—modified by additional provisions against computer offenses and credit card fraud—until spring 1986. The final step was primarily formal. The House sent the bill to the state chamber where it was approved.

Outline of This Book: Theory and Research

Following this introductory section, Part II of this book deals with theoretical and methodological issues. In Chapter 2 we distinguish several sociological approaches to the explanation of criminal justice legislation: functionalist versus conflict group or action theory, and Marxist versus pluralist or differentiation theory. We associate four competing approaches with examples from criminal justice and socio-legal studies. Basic patterns of our case demonstrate the limits of functionalist approaches at the outset. They suggest that it is fruitful to focus on the detailed analysis of the political process, on the action orientation of central participants in the legislation, and on the conditions and effects of action rationales and strategies. We introduce cognitive mapping as a methodological tool to measure these rationales. This approach develops and differentiates, in the process of a case study, a pluralist, action-oriented conflict theory of criminal law making.

Part III presents the empirical analysis. After giving an overview of the claims-making process in two crucial news magazines, we analyze cognitive maps of commissioners and politicians, comparing them by types of decision makers, by phases of the claims-making and legislative processes, by situations, and by offenses they address. Comparisons of maps along these dimensions allow for numerous conclusions concerning the rationales and action strategies of decision makers. We organized the empirical part by phases of the process. This is justified since several important independent variables—such as institutional context, politicization, and publicity—vary with the phase under consideration.

The first phase is characterized by increasingly massive claims making by mass media, criminal justice practitioners, politicians, and academics, leading to the economic crime debate at the 1972 Meeting of the German Lawyers Association (Chapter 3). The second phase is dominated by the expert commission. Our analysis is based on intensive interviews with almost all commissioners and on the commission reports. For comparative reasons we also include the analysis of expert hearings from the later legislative phase in this analysis (Chapter 4). In the third phase the Department of Justice promulgates proposals for two bills against economic crime. Our analysis of this phase is based on a comprehensive analysis of the archives of the German Industry Federation (*Bund der Deutschen Industrie*) and interviews with representatives of lobby organizations and decision makers in the Justice Department. The final legislative phase is analyzed on the basis of three types of data: parliamentary minutes of decisive plenary and committee sessions; interviews with representatives and decision makers from the ministerial bureaucracies of different states; and our own observation of a public hearing held by the judicial committee of the *Bundestag* on issues of the Second Law Against Economic Crime (Chapter 5).

The discussion of individual phases is followed by a comprehensive analysis of a sample of 94 different cognitive maps from different phases. We identify relations between several situative and structural variables and formal and substantive features of the cognitive maps (Chapter 6).

In Part IV, the final part, we first draw conclusions from our empirical case study along the theoretical dimensions developed earlier

(Chapter 7). We then present an explicit though preliminary comparison between the cases of criminal law making in the United States and in the Federal Republic of Germany during recent decades. We identify commonalities and differences and we discuss potential explanations for both (Chapter 8).

Part II
Theory and Methods in the Study of White-Collar Crime Legislation

Chapter 2
Rationalities, Communication, and Power: Theoretical Perspectives and Methods

The choice of the Second Law Against Economic Crime for our study of white-collar crime legislation was driven by empirical and theoretical concerns. First, this legislation was part of the most substantial effort against economic crime undertaken in German history. Second, since the legislative process was still ongoing when the project began, memories among participants were fresh and reliable. Third, the decisions passed in this process had been prepared by extensive commission and parliamentary work, which provided us with sufficient material to reconstruct the legislative process.

Fourth, and most important, the case is well suited to confront different sociological theories on the emergence and development of criminal law with empirical reality. A case study, of course, cannot verify or rigorously falsify complex theories, particularly if these theories refer to long-term patterns of change. Even so, a case study can suggest modifications and alternative hypotheses. It can also point to contradictions among overly streamlined theoretical assumptions and help to develop further research questions.

In this chapter we discuss different theories on the making of criminal law and relate them to basic features of our case and to findings in the literature. We confront conflict group with functionalist theories and Marxist with differentiation theoretical approaches. We first outline theories that are differentiation and conflict group oriented. We then discuss functionalist approaches that have long been prominent in the sociology of criminal law making. While some features of our case could be used to support Marxist-functionalist approaches, others pose challenges to this tradition. We finally identify rationalities (that is, action orientations), power, and communication as basic theoretical concepts that need to be taken into consideration in an empirical study of criminal law making against economic crime and develop our methodological approach accordingly.

Mapping the Theoretical Field

Our research problem, the explanation of economic crime legislation in advanced capitalist societies, can most conveniently be placed in a strand of recent research on legal change in welfare states. In his internationally comparative investigation of the development of welfare states, Jens Alber (1982) distinguishes four theoretical traditions in sociology by applying two dichotomized dimensions: (1) Marxist versus pluralist (or differentiation) theory, and (2) functionalist versus conflict group (or action) theory. Each of these traditions tries to explain the origin and expansion of the welfare state and the laws by which these states are characterized. Alber tests the validity of these theory types with comprehensive, internationally comparative statistical data. He finds that differentiation and conflict group theories can best explain the origin and development of modern welfare law.

Criminal law is the negative complement to welfare law. While welfare systems attempt to control and stabilize social order through the application of positive sanctions such as monetary benefits and services, criminal justice seeks to effect social control through negative sanctions such as fines, probation, imprisonment, or death. Each of the theoretical approaches Alber distinguishes, we contend, can be applied not only to welfare law but also to criminal law. In this book we test if differentiation and conflict group theories also best explain the development of *criminal law* in welfare states.

Classical approaches to the genesis of criminal law vary across the four theory types. Confronting them with results from recent empirical research and the basic facts of our case helps us select for our case study the best suited conceptual framework, methodology, and instruments of data gathering.

Differentiation and Conflict Group Theory

In his sociology of law, Max Weber (1978, pp. 641–900) provides an early sociological discussion of legal development that extends to the stage of welfare states. His discussion can be fruitfully applied to the spread of white-collar crime legislation in the late twentieth century. Weberian sociology of law suggests hypotheses concerning the conditions and consequences of this spread.

Weber describes the differentiation and development of law in the context of the "rise of Western rationalism" (Schluchter 1981). He provides a typology of law according to his famous dimensions of rational versus irrational and formal versus substantive. "Rational" refers to legal rules being part of a logical and gapless system, "formal" to the exclusion of extra-legal criteria from legal decision making (Trubek 1972).

A closer look at the types of formal versus substantive rationality of law reveals opposing social ideals and terms of liberty (Winckelmann 1976, p. 120). *Formal rationality* is the principle of classical bourgeois law. Its social ideal consists of the absence of value judgments and the maximum amount of individual freedom for economic, social, political, and personal action. In *substantive rationality* the creation and interpretation of legal terms take place with continuing reference to concrete problems and conflicts within the given social order. The measure of rationality is the reasonability of the proposed social models. The social ideal is the welfare state's guarantee for security, peace, and equal opportunity for the majority of the population. Formal rationality is concerned with liberty in the sense of the libertarian bourgeois state. Substantive rationality conceives of liberty in the sociological sense, the main impediment of which is the legalized differentiation of property (Weber 1978, pp. 812–814).

Weber thus sees an inescapable contradiction between the abstract formalism of legal logic and the need for the fulfillment of substantive demands. Under conditions of legal formalism the legal apparatus functions like a technically rational machine. It allows a maximum amount of freedom for actors and the rational calculation or prediction of the consequences of purposeful social actions. Weber sees western law of the modern bourgeois state as moving toward formal rationality, leaving the two types of irrational law and substantive rational law behind. Yet the rise of formal rationality, in combination with the unequal distribution of economic means and power, implies a threat to substantive ideals of justice. Since the ideals of the welfare state are opposed to legal formalism, Weber (1978, pp. 882–883) predicts legal substantivation and, closely related, particularization (i.e., anti-formalist tendencies) for the development of legal systems in welfare states. Writing in the early twentieth century, Weber finds indications for a renewed turn toward substantive rationality.

The spheres of . . . special laws . . . [are] predominantly defined along substantive or functional criteria, and it is only under certain circumstances that applicability is governed by formal tests. Many of these modern laws are also combined with special courts and procedures of their own. In the first place they have been a result of the occupational differentiation and the increasing attention which commercial and industrial pressure groups have obtained for themselves. What they expect from these particularistic arrangements is that their legal affairs will be handled by specialized experts. The second cause which has played an increasingly important role in most recent times, has been the desire to eliminate the formalities of normal legal procedure for the sake of a settlement that would be both expeditious and better adapted to the concrete case. In practice, this trend signifies a weakening of legal formalism out of considerations of substantive expediency. (Weber 1978, pp. 881–882)

Weber's comments on the economic law of his time are confirmed by contemporary observations of criminal law. For example, internal differentiation of criminal law is expressed in the ever-increasing flood of criminal provisions outside the criminal code, especially in laws regulating the economy, environmental law, labor law, credit law, trade law, and stock exchange law (Schick 1981). This process results in increasing conflicts between principles of criminal law—such as justice, crime control, retribution—and the rationales of the sectors regulated by these special laws.

The *institutions* of criminal justice undergo a parallel development of internal differentiation. Special police units, prosecutorial offices, and special court chambers are created for a diversity of areas including economic or white-collar offenses. While these specialized institutions are meant to lead to more efficient law enforcement, they may also highlight conflicts between specifically legal criteria of formal rationality and substantive rationales of the target spheres of legal control (e.g., economic criteria). Conflicts between economic and legal rationales in the implementation and legislation of white-collar law are one example (Bussmann and Lüdemann 1992; Mann, Wheeler, and Sarat 1980; Savelsberg 1987). It is not surprising then that the dominant conflict line in our case study of economic crime legislation emerged between jurisprudents of economic versus criminal law and between departments and committees for economic versus criminal justice affairs throughout the process of consultation and legislation. Only in the last stage of the process did the conflict line move along party lines.

Weber does not assume that legal change, for example substantivation and particularization, occurs as a well-synchronized and quasi-automatic adaptation to socio-structural change. Instead he identifies concrete carrier groups of legal substantivation, for example legal clients (see quotation above). Other carrier groups are subordinate classes that pose

new demands for a "social law" to be based on such emotionally colored ethical postulates as "justice" and "human dignity," directed against the pure business morality having arisen with the modern class problem. (Weber 1978, p. 886)

The legal profession constitutes a third force aiming at the consideration of substantive criteria in legal decision making. Lawyers feel their social status to be endangered by formal-rational law that reduces them to

a slot machine into which one just drops the facts (plus the fee) in order to have it spew out the decision (plus the opinion). (Weber 1978, p. 886)

Weber's theory of the formation of law in modern welfare states thus integrates elements of differentiation and action (or conflict group) theory. It directs our attention to specialized laws, as well as institutions in modern law, associated with new forms of particularism and discretion, and to specific carrier groups of this process.

Weber's ideas have influenced important strands of current sociological research on the making of criminal law. This is especially true for his contention that power and domination determine the varying success of social groups in the development of legal forms. Hans Haferkamp (1980, 1983, 1984), a recent German sociologist of criminal law, for example, applies Weber's line of thought to recent decades of research on the making of criminal law. Haferkamp's review of recent literature indicates that many researchers have been interested in the impact of diverse interest groups on criminal justice legislation: the upper class (e.g., Carson 1974; Hall 1952; Schumann 1974); the middle class (e.g., Arzt 1976; Schumann 1974); and organizations of professional groups, social control agencies, and moral crusaders (e.g., Akers 1975; Becker 1973; Blankenburg and Treiber 1975; Chambliss and Seidman 1982; Gusfield 1967; Matthes 1964; Quinney 1975; Roby 1975). Haferkamp finds that the interest groups considered in the literature are distinguished along various dimensions. This diversity of dimensions renders it difficult to draw generalizing conclusions from these case studies. Haferkamp thus reorganizes the groups discussed in these studies within a common context of power and domination. A meta-analysis of these studies then suggests that criminal law making is determined largely by social groups that can be distinguished by different fields of domination (functional sectors of society) and levels of domination. These groups compete with each other, define and articulate their norm-interests, and organize their realization (Haferkamp 1980, pp. 53–56).

The conditions under which groups compete change through time. Increasing functional differentiation results in the growing dependency of modern societies on the achievements of ever more specialized populations. This development results in a redistribution of societal power away from formerly dominant groups and classes toward new social groups. Among the latter are the representatives of welfare bureaucracies or "new little masters" (Haferkamp 1984, p. 124)—at least in European welfare states.

If Haferkamp's assumption is valid that the development of criminal law making reflects the distribution of power and domination between different groups in society, the dissolution and redistribution of domination he observes would be followed by a liberalization of criminal law or a redistribution of the chances of members of different social groups to become criminalized (Aubert 1952). This prediction is confirmed by recent partial decriminalization in Germany, especially in the area of sex and morality (e.g., abortion and homosexual behavior), and by current attempts to criminalize previously protected groups (e.g., white-collar offenders) and sectors (Schick 1981).

Haferkamp's prognosis concurs with that of Weber in important respects. There should be a decrease in formal legal equality and freedom, identified by Weber as the basis for the free play of societal power, and in the resulting societal structures of social inequality. In fact, formal legal equality is currently being replaced by a fight over different substantive rationales. Weber and Haferkamp discuss welfare rationales that aim at the achievement of actual (sociological) equality. This equality consists of equal opportunities for members of society to obtain goods and to avoid such restrictions as the criminalization and sanctioning of behavior by state authorities. This equality has a complementary side: it results in attempts to criminalize previously powerful groups and to establish specialized legal codes and institutions to deal with particular types of offenders, including white-collar or economic offenders. Concrete interest groups, gaining power and domination from the process of societal differentiation, are the driving forces of this legal change.

Yet, in the fight for the pursuance of substantive rationales, considerations different from those with welfare may prevail, as we shall see in the following sections. Max Weber was very much aware of this. He argued that the fight for the admission of substantive rationales, justified with concern for welfare of the lower classes, may instead benefit traditional power groups, especially under conditions of a conservative judiciary and where men predominate in groups of decision makers (e.g., in rape cases) (Weber 1978, p. 893). Substantive rationales may thus aim, for example, to protect interests of established status groups, advance technological progress, promote economic growth, or assist particular large corporations. The latter criteria are especially likely to persist if traditional and economic power groups maintain some of their power potentials or gain new access to power (see Calavita and Pontell 1990 on finance capitalism) despite the access that previously subordinate groups gain to other sources of power (e.g., through representation in parliament or the establishment of welfare bureau-cracies). "Multiple social hierarchies" or "diverse status systems" are useful terms to describe this situation, as suggested by Vilhelm Aubert (1952) in his article on "white-collar crime and social structure."

What kinds of legal decisions are substantively rational depends then on the particular frame of reference. We shall talk about *rationalities* throughout this book when we mean sets of arguments or beliefs that reflect reasoning within different frames of reference or different sets of substantive criteria. These criteria may be defined by social actors distinguished along vertical and horizontal forms of social differentia-tion. We shall further refer to lines of argument that reflect such rationalities as *argumentations*.

Functionalist Approaches

Most prominent studies on the genesis and development of criminal law are functionalist. Hagan (1980) distinguishes two types of func-tionalist approaches to criminal law. The first type, "moral functional-ism," refers to societal needs as reference points for functional analysis. Criminal laws are seen as "good" solutions to socioeconomic problems. The second type, "moral Marxism," refers to class-specific functions of law and regards criminal laws as "bad" solutions to socioeconomic problems.

Functional analysis, especially moral functionalism, has a long tradi-tion in sociology. It aims, according to Malinowski (1926, pp. 132–133), "at the *explanation* of anthropological facts . . . *through the function and role* they play within the general cultural system" (italics added). Mal-inowski expresses the central strategy of functionalism: "explanation through function." According to Radcliffe-Brown (1935, pp. 395–396), another classical representative of this theory tradition, "the function of any repetitive activity, such as the punishment of a crime . . ., consists in the role it plays in social life as a whole, and consequently in its contribution to the maintenance of structural continuity." Thus, ac-cording to functionalists, social facts serve a function for the mainte-nance of the social system and their existence can thus be explained.

In classical sociology, Émile Durkheim represents this tradition most prominently. Durkheim believed that law changes from repressive to restitutive, and that punishment becomes ever more lenient when the process of functional differentiation creates new demands for social integration (Durkheim 1899/1900). One of Durkheim's most promi-nent contemporary successors, Donald Black (1976, 1987), predicts a decrease in punishment and an increase in restitutive law naturally resulting from changing social structures. Black's work, however, is more complex than moral functionalism; it also contains elements of John Hagan's "moral Marxism." Changes in power structures automatically lead to a changing practice of a law that adjusts to the needs of powerful new élites.

Other authors stand more unambiguously in the Marxist functionalist tradition. Rusche and Kirchheimer's (1939) famous book *Social Structure and Punishment* is the most prominent classical example. The authors attempt to explain the development of criminal punishment from the early middle ages into modernity from the perspective of historical materialism. According to their central thesis, "every *system of production tends to discover* punishments which correspond to its productive relationships" (Rusche and Kirchheimer 1939, p. 5; italics added). Similarly, Hall (1952) explains the creation of theft law in sixteenth-century England through the need to secure rapidly expanding economic exchange relations and the transport of goods in early industrialization. Hall's interpretation is supported by Chambliss's (1964) analysis of changes of the "law of vagrancy" in the early sixteenth century. Both studies, however, can be reinterpreted in the tradition of interest group theory. In both cases the interests of new powerful economic classes and interest groups were identical with the functional needs of the emerging industrial-capitalist system (for a recent dispute on Marxist interpretations of vagrancy law see Chambliss 1989 versus Adler 1989).

A group of Austrian scholars have recently followed in the steps of Rusche and Kirchheimer. Pilgram and Steinert (1975) explain the directions of the Austrian criminal code reform through changing conditions of production and reproduction of the 1960s. They oppose welfare interpretations of liberalizations by leading criminal code reformers. Instead, they argue that functional needs of the economy had been the driving force of the code reform. A coincidence of economic growth and demographic stagnation created needs for a greater labor force. They interpret the liberal code reform as an attempt to reduce dequalifications, especially of the young labor force, by avoiding incarceration (Steinert 1978).

Serious critiques, however, have been directed against functionalism (Hempel 1958; but see Chambliss and Seidman 1982, p. 148). First, the problem of functional relics is unresolved. Even if criminal law norms and institutions have emerged under conditions of functional need, social facts develop their own dynamics and become independent from the functional needs that have contributed to their creation.

Second, functionalist approaches do not deal with the problem of functional equivalents. Functions can always be fulfilled by a diversity of potential institutionalizations. For example, cashless systems of money transfer can be secured by creating criminal law provisions against the abuse of credit cards or by obliging banks to introduce preventive security technologies. Functionalists cannot explain why a *particular* institution has emerged.

Third, functionalist approaches use holistic and reifying formulations (e.g., Rusche and Kirchheimer's "system of production [which] tends to discover"). They overlook the fact that functional needs—if they are to have any impact on social institutions—must be processed in several steps. They must be: (1) perceived by actors; (2) translated into individual or group interests (see Hagan 1980); (3) articulated and directed at political and legal decision makers; and (4) perceived by decision makers and translated into binding decisions.

Finally, functionalist approaches are characterized by a methodological problem. They typically try to prove their arguments by citing ostensibly supportive examples and do not search for falsifying cases that would lead to the modification or rejection of overly streamlined theoretical assumptions. The history of criminal law making against economic offenses in Germany provides numerous examples that could support the plausibility of Marxist functionalist hypotheses listed above. For example, the introduction of provisions against the misuse of credit cards and computer crime can be interpreted in just the way in which Hall (1952) and Chambliss (1964) explain the creation of sixteenth-century laws against theft and vagrancy: as a means to secure informational and economic exchange processes and thereby further productivity and the advancement of modern technologies. New provisions against investment fraud, that is, the false or insufficient information of investors, react to new needs of the investment market. The amount of capital in the hands of members of the upper middle class has been increasing. For example, professionals with only minimal experience in capital investment were easily victimized by fraudulent investment companies. The new law seemed necessary to prevent such victimization and thus to maintain the willingness of these groups to invest and satisfy the demands from the capital market.

Yet our case of economic crime legislation also shows serious problems with functionalist interpretations of law making. They fail to recognize (1) contradictions and differentiations along a variety of dimensions within sectors of society. They also do not address (2) the distinction between perceived and articulated interests on the one hand and functional needs on the other, as well as the complex relation between them.

1. Criminal law norms directed at the economy affect different social classes, especially employers and employees, in different ways. Different sectors in the economy, different regions in the country, and the

organizations that represent functionally, segmentarily, regionally, or class-level differentiated subsystems or subgroups of the economic system also experience different impacts. This situation leads to predictable patterns of conflict and alliance. In computer crime, the conflict is between employers and customers on one side and employees, for example computer programmers, on the other. Regarding price fixing, the mining industry suffers from bid rigging in the construction sector. Subsidy-related crime, frequent in the agricultural sector supported by the European Community, causes higher consumer prices particularly felt in highly urbanized and industrialized regions.

At the same time, surprising coalitions in the economic sector appear where conflict might be expected. In the case of price fixing, for example, industry associations and unions formed a hidden coalition. Both were concerned about the survival of numerous construction firms that worked with a small margin of profit. The expected deterrent effect of a bid rigging proposition would drive many of them into bankruptcy.

2. The price fixing example also helps to illustrate the potential conflict between perceived and articulated interests of organized units of one economic sector and the actual productivity of that sector or the economy as a whole. It may be true that the proposition against bid rigging might cause the bankruptcy of some construction firms. On the other hand, as economics professor Finsinger argued at a hearing of the judicial committee of the *Bundestag,* it would force the construction industry to adapt to changed market conditions and to accept technical innovation, which, in turn, would have positive impacts on modern technology sectors.

The proposed criminalization of bid rigging was defeated in the lawmaking process. Concrete interests within the economic sector prevailed against more abstract and general economic arguments. At least three explanations come to mind:

1. *Rationalities.* Individual and organized interests and rationales can be more easily articulated than long-term systemic functional needs.
2. *Communications.* Concrete communication networks and interest relations link groups with immediate interests and political decision makers.
3. *Power.* Sanctions against lawmakers by actors with specific interests (e.g., withdrawal of funding and votes), rather than more abstract economic consequences, are more likely to occur within the legislative period.

Power and Rationalities: Marxism and the Theory of Social Action

Theoretical considerations and the basic features of our empirical case suggest that social action or conflict group theory, as reflected in the work of Weber and Haferkamp, prevails over the functionalist approach. Yet, some of the illustrations of Marxist hypotheses seem to suggest modifications of hypotheses that are derived from those authors' differentiation (or pluralistic) theoretical approach. While Haferkamp's "new little masters" may have gained power in the welfare state, old masters (e.g., powerful corporations and industry associations) continue to have considerable influence on criminal legislation (Aubert 1952). Furthermore, several current trends oppose Haferkamp's pluralistic assumptions: the weakness of labor unions following the decline of old industries and the growth of international capital and increasing international exchange of money, services, and goods. The resulting supra-systemic power can affect decisions in political systems, as shown in studies of absentee-owned corporations. Power potentials organized beyond the limits of a municipality or nation state are more likely to be anticipated by political decision makers than power potentials confined to the limits of the system (Savelsberg 1980, pp. 114–132). Examples from Canadian economic crime legislation illustrate this general argument (Hagan and Parker 1985).

Empirical studies that combine a Marxist and a conflict group or action theoretical perspective identify further conditions under which corporate interest groups prevail over the "new little masters." Gerald Turkel (1980), for example, investigates the impacts of capital concentration on the legislation of subsidies law. He shows how formal legal systems that were highly functional under a free competition market economy (Turner 1981, pp. 318–351) became dysfunctional under high capital concentration. Consequently, substantive criteria and particularization intrude on the formal legal order, as predicted by Weber. According to Turkel, however, this situation favors particularly powerful actors. In his case study, both the federal administration and the U.S. Congress reacted to Lockheed Aircraft's financial crisis with a law that offered subsidies in such universalistic terms as to legitimize them. But it in fact targeted specifically the needs of one company.

Turkel explains this particularization through the "privatization" of the public sector. The state as a stockholder becomes dependent on particular economic enterprises. In critical economic situations the state is also expected to intervene in favor of dominant sectors of the economy, given the high visibility of the resulting bankruptcies. As a result, the legal discourse expands beyond Weber's term of legal formality to include technical criteria and political standards.

In sum, Turkel's analysis confirms Weber's prognosis of the intrusion of substantive criteria of rationality into formal legal systems and of particularization (i.e., loss of universalistic orientation). Here, however, the explanatory factors are not functional differentiation and the domination of "new little masters" but the newly increased power of economic actors. The importance of considering different "rationalities" and identifying Aubert's "multiple social hierarchies" and "multiple status systems" is again confirmed. At the same time, Turkel's analysis supports action or conflict-group theory, for the interests of the powerful do not prevail without intervention but must be fought for in negotiations with and within the political sector.

Power and Communication: The Pursuit of Interest in Social Action

Decision making in the context of criminal justice legislation is social action, oriented toward ideal or material interests (Weber). The types and distribution of interests are determined by economic and social structures. The more functionally differentiated such structures are (which they are to a very high degree in modern societies), the more diverse and interdependent are the interests of different groups and sectors of society. Decisions that bind all members of society therefore concern a diversity of more or less conflicting interests, interests of societal groups and units within the political-administrative system. These interests may be communicated to decision makers or anticipated by them. Interests have a better chance to be considered by decision makers (i.e., their carriers are more influential), when carriers of interest have better access to decision makers through communicative processes, or when interests of carriers are anticipated by decision makers. These chances increase the more decision makers expect to feel the reactions of interest groups to their decisions, that is, the more powerful interest groups are. Concepts that must be considered and integrated in an action theoretical model are ideal and material interests; conflict; communication and power; and, finally, decision making that constitutes criminalizations and the rationalities on which they are based.

Laws and their enforcement thus do not always directly reflect conflicting interests. They need to be first perceived and then considered relevant by decision makers. Interests need to be *anticipated* or *communicated,* before they can be considered in decision making. Decision makers must judge if the consideration or nonconsideration of particular interests impacts on their intended purposes.

The term *power* describes the chances of actors or societal systems to be considered by decision makers. "Power" is a central concept both within political sociology and the sociology of crime and delinquency (Becker 1973). Unfortunately, the debate about power has been characterized by a considerable degree of terminological confusion. Power has been understood as the superior "ability to make rules and apply them to other people" (Becker 1973, p. 17). On the other hand, law has been defined as a "mechanism of the practice of power" (Carson 1974) or as a type of power, "legal power," through which people try to gain control over those mechanisms that secure norm conformity beyond the limits of their culturally homogeneous group (Turk 1976). Others are concerned with the impacts of law on power: the sanctioning of subordinate groups as a mechanism for the stabilization of power structures (Popitz 1968) or the transformation of relatively unstable power relations into relatively stable relations of domination through legal norms (Haferkamp 1980; Lautmann 1975). In these debates "power" is used in a number of ways. It is seen as identical with law or law is understood as a dimension of power. Power is regarded as a condition of law or law is considered a condition of power through feedback processes. Or law is understood as a transformer of power into domination. In our analysis we are interested in power as an independent variable contributing to the genesis of criminal statutes.

An important complement of power that requires consideration in the study of criminal legislation is its close relation to the concepts of information and the perception of reality. Chances for communication are a decisive factor for the preparation of criminalizing norms (Becker 1973). Sociological discussions on the interrelation between communication and power have stressed the relational property of power. Power is not the characteristic of its carrier. It constitutes a relation between different actors. Power, for this reason, can only function when it is perceived, and therefore depends on the transmission of perception, and thus on communication.

Some authors believe that communication as such is more effective than power in directing social change (Deutsch 1971). Be this as it may, power and communication can be partly substituted by each other. Etzioni argues:

If a message is less clear but more enforced or less enforced but more clear, similar results may be obtained. But such substitutions are limited in scope; when faced with resistance, the clearest communication will be useless unless it is backed with sufficient power, and a large application of power will yield little action if the control centers receive vague or conflicting information. (1968, p. 336)

In general, access to channels of communication can be understood as a necessary condition for the use of power or as a partial substitute for power. Considering the importance of communicative processes for the outcome of decision making, we analyze comprehensively the communication flows and networks between a central association of industry and representatives of the political system in this study.

Rationalities in Action and Structural Conditions

The previous discussion nourishes skepticism toward functionalist approaches no matter if they are left or right, if they aim at functional criteria of societies or the economic sector. Instead we suggest an action theoretical analysis of political decision making that creates societal and criminal legal reality—an analysis of the perception of reality and resulting rationalities on which those decisions are based. The situational and structural conditions of these perceptions and rationales need to be empirically identified.

Such a theoretical approach is not blind to the importance of interests. To the contrary, political action is understood as oriented toward ideal and material interests. It is also not blind toward societal and organizational structures. These must be identified as conditions of decision making. For these reasons our program is also not idealistic. It has nothing in common with what Stangl (1985) calls "naive action theory." It neither assumes the primacy of economics nor rejects this primacy without further analysis. Instead it aims at empirical examination. Our program also does not assume a political rationality oriented toward policy goals. This assumption too becomes an object of empirical analysis. Our approach does assume that decision making is rational only in the context of particular social spheres and with regard to specific criteria of rationality, goals, and interests. It is a central concern of this analysis to identify those decision-making rationales.

Finally our approach does not overlook conflicts. It rejects approaches that assume a priori that societal, economic, or other system-specific interests have impacts on law without the slightest intervention of social actors, and rejects as well approaches that deductively conclude that criminal justice and criminal justice legislation are protected by a high degree of autonomy from societal and group interests (Waldmann 1979).

Questions concerning the degree and conditions under which interest groups versus state autonomy prevail will be answered separately for different phases of the political process; for the particular agencies involved; for the type of program, proposition, or bill; and for the particular societal groups concerned. Specific hypotheses formulated by

Blankenburg and Treiber (1975) become relevant. For example, the more enclosed an administrative action system, the greater the influence of the implementing agency and the more likely a shift of conflicts from program development to the parliamentary decision-making process. The lower the politicization of an issue in the general public, the higher the influence of the implementing agency. Further, the politicization of an issue itself is understood as dependent on three variables: first, the presence of organized and conflictual interest groups whose status is threatened; second, the chances that "moral entrepreneurs" appear and conduct political "crusades" (Becker 1973); third, the chances that an active public may develop and produce conflicts through institutional interpreters.

In sum, we do not discuss the political system as a black box. The role of actors in the legislative process is explicitly included in the analysis. Only in this way can central questions for the empirical reality of legislation be answered. For example:

- Under what conditions do which interest groups have what chances to be influential in criminal justice legislation?
- Through what mechanisms is such influence exerted?
- To what degree and when will interests be anticipated, and when must they be manifestly documented?
- How are interests perceived and reflected in patterns of decision making and legitimation?
- What role do situational versus structural conditions of decision making play?
- What influence do interest and target groups have when distinguished by the socioeconomic status of potential offenders and victims?

Answers to these questions are likely to vary by stages of the claims-making and law-making process. The following chapters will discuss each of these stages in the search for differentiated answers. First, however, some brief methodological comments are warranted.

Methods of Research: Documents, Interviews, and Cognitive Maps

Because this book is an in-depth study of one case of criminal justice legislation, the research is not suited for rigorous hypothesis testing. A case study is suited, however, to question overly streamlined empirical conclusions and theoretical models that are widespread in scholarly literature and in everyday beliefs. The results can thus challenge theoretical models and can be compared to those of other case studies. Second, the case includes larger numbers of units of analysis on a lower level of aggregation. It seems possible, therefore, to use data on units to assess theoretical propositions. For example, the legislation under study includes a diversity of provisions, some of which target entrepreneurs, others employees. It also seems possible to conduct analyses using our sample of 97 cognitive maps, which we identify for numerous situations and actors and for several stages of the law-making process (see below).

The method for gathering data varies by stages. We analyzed leading news magazines and documents from the commission of experts, from the archives of lobbying organizations, and from the legislative process. We conducted intensive interviews with legislators, administrators, lobbyists, and commissioners. We give specific information on the methods applied and materials used to analyze each stage in the law-making process in the relevant chapters below.

Central to our interest was the analysis of the structures of the actors' argumentation. We used this analysis to identify different actors' motives and underlying political interests and rationalities. For this purpose we applied the cognitive mapping approach developed by Robert Axelrod and others (see Axelrod 1976). A cognitive map presents the assumptions an actor makes about a limited problem and describes the structure of that actor's causal assumptions or argumentations. These maps consist of two basic elements: concepts (variables) and assumed positive or negative causal relations. These relations are represented on the maps by arrows in a presentation that is comparable to path analysis. The procedure can be distinguished by four central steps: the coding of the text (document or interview); the creation of a concept dictionary; the creation of relationship cards; and the construction of cognitive maps.

We followed the coding procedures developed by Bonham and Shapiro (1984). The four steps were executed as follows:

1. First the text was read by two coders. During the second reading they identified causal relations. Terms relevant to these assumed relations were marked by circles. Causal relations were marked with arrows in the direction of the causal dependence. The arrows were coded with a +, for positive relations, with a − for negative relations. The intercoder reliability was about 90 percent. The coders reached agreement for the remaining cases.

2. After the coding we established a concept dictionary. We listed all terms that express the same idea on cards. We then gave each card a title that expressed the common concept (variable) and gave each separate concept under that heading an identification number. Related

concepts were marked by the same letter: conditions for the behavior of entrepreneurs (A); price-fixing behavior of entrepreneurs and related terms (B); reactions of firms to sanctions and norms (C); impacts of entrepreneurs' behavior (D); norms against price fixing (E); actions of the criminal justice system (F); impacts of norms and the behavior of control agents (G); goods to be protected (H); and reactions of the public (I).

Group A, for example, contained four concepts (A1, A2, A3, and A4). Under each concept heading the terms are summarized in such a way that they can be re-identified in the text. (I24 in front of a term in the concept dictionary means document number I, page 24.) A number behind the term refers to the decision maker by whom it was used. (C1 feeling of guilt 2 means concept C1 expressed by actor number 2.)

3. We then established the relationship cards. Each causal relation was listed on a card that was marked by the relevant concept number as well as the direction of the causal relations (e.g., E1, G1+ means the more severe the sanctions, the higher the deterrence effect). In addition, the codes of the source and the speaker were noted on each relationship card (e.g., 2-I19 means speaker 2 on page 19 of document I). The relationship cards were organized by documents and within documents by speakers.

4. We deduced the cognitive maps directly from the relationship file for each speaker. Concept names and identification codes are organized from left (independent variables) to right (dependent variables). The arrows between the concepts and the respective variables are marked by the source and the sign for the causal direction. Each causal relation in the map can therefore easily be traced back to the original document.

Having pursued this analysis for important documents of the consulting and legislative processes, we established an electronic data file with individual maps as units of analysis. Variables included concern the structural and situational context in which each map was produced (independent) and the maps' substantive and formal features (dependent).

The cognitive mapping approach is a reliable tool to identify cognitive or argumentation structures. High intercoder reliability was reached after intense coder training that helped to establish the coders' common understanding of the issues under consideration and of truly causal relations (as opposed to tautological, definitional, or temporal relations). This approach is sometimes used to understand the cognitions of decision makers directly. However, this is not adequate for analyzing the political setting under consideration. Statements of politicians or any other negotiating actors do not naively represent their cognitions, and they often do not just represent their individual concerns. Instead they tend to be the result of collective negotiation processes in a political party, a wing of that party, a faction, or a ministry. In addition, politicians' argumentations, that is, their lines of argument, may be influenced by strategic considerations or legitimation needs. We therefore speak of argumentation structures rather than cognitive structures. The analysis of these structures, however, and their comparison with those on other issues or in other situations allow for conclusions on underlying (covert) motives of representatives or their factions. Sets of arguments, when strategically adapted to different issues or situations, may not be consistent with each other. We are particularly interested in identifying such treacherous contradictions.

Part III
The Case Study: From Claims Making to Legislation

Chapter 3
The Social Problem of Economic Crime, Claims Making, and Motivating the Political Process

Conditions for Economic Crime, Control Agencies, and Measurement

Several events need to occur before politicians, legislatures, and public administrators react to social problems. Many expect functional problems of the economy, the political order, or the system of social control to initiate state responses. Yet such problems need to be registered— for example by institutionalized societal bookkeeping systems such as crime and court statistics in criminal justice studies. And societal groups must effectively claim that problems exist before political action is taken.

Extensive research in the study of social problems has demonstrated that the making of claims and their success in the public arena are often independent of both functional problems and institutionalized problem measurement (Schneider 1985). Selective control of the media of information and political structures may cause basic functional problems never to gain a broad public forum, as the study of nondecision making has shown (Bachrach and Baratz 1970; Crenson 1971). Other problems become hotly debated issues even though their actual occurrence has hardly increased. Structural problems and claims making may initate political and administrative responses. This is particularly so when the problem definition promises political gain and when it fits existing administrative schemes.

This chapter briefly discusses the structural conditions of the economic crime problem and then investigates claims making against economic offenses in mass media and in the legal profession. This leads to the question of which claims enter the political realm and how they get transformed in the political decision-making process. We demonstrate that claims against white-collar crime aim at powerful offenders victimizing simple people, while actors in the political process are likely to use the politically attractive "white-collar" label to criminalize occupational crimes of low-level employees while letting the powerful go unchallenged (on similar reasoning for the U.S. Department of Justice see Simon and Swart 1984).

The structural opportunities for economic or white-collar crime are improving. Important factors are the tertiarization of the economy, that is, its shift from industrial production to services (for finance capitalism in the United States see Calavita and Pontell 1990), and the related increase of the white-collar class (Kaiser 1980, p. 495). The long-lasting structural decline of established industries may also contribute to rising economic crime in that it increasingly restricts legitimate opportunities for established businesses (Coleman 1987, pp. 427–431). Furthermore, the implementation of new technologies, especially in data and information processing, creates new opportunities for illegal behavior while control strategies lag behind technological innovation (Tiedemann 1976, vol. 2, p. 149). Further pressure toward increasing white-collar crime is attributed to cyclical recessions of economic activity and to structural impediments to economic development experienced after the "oil crisis" and with the "second industrial revolution."

While illegitimate opportunities increase, the control potentials of enforcement agencies decrease. First, many new offenses were not defined in the codes of civil law countries. An example is theft of computer software. The definition of theft is aimed at the appropriation of movable goods. Since computer programs are not movable goods, their theft was not covered by the provisions against theft in the German criminal code (para. 242 *Strafgesetzbuch*) until the 1986 code reform. Second, numerous crimes are committed from within corporations with increasingly complex organizational structures. This process inhibits successful attribution of criminal liability to concrete offenders (Coffee 1981; Doig, Phillips, and Manson 1984).

Time series data on the development of white-collar crime in West Germany are available for the short period of 1974 to 1981. They are based on the Federal Registry of White-Collar Offenses (*Bundesweite Erfassung von Wirtschaftsstraftaten*), gathered for a limited time period by researchers of the Max Planck Institute for International and Comparative Criminal Law in Freiburg. This registration is an aggregation of data from prosecutorial files for all states of the Republic. Different indicators show different trends during these years. The number of procedures increased from 2,800 (1974) to 3,727 (1977), then declined to 3,102 (1981). The amount of damage registered increased from a value of 1,380 million German marks (1974) to 5,477 million (1978), then dropped to 3,592 million (1981). The number of individual cases covered by prosecutorial procedures increased from 51,150 (1974) to 145,209 (1980) to then drop to 127,843 (1981) (Liebl 1984, pp. 26, 128, and Tables 44, 48, and 49). The development of damage per procedure is from 0.6 million German marks in 1974 to 1.9 million (1978) to 1.3 million (1981). Overall, we observe a considerable increase in prosecutorial records of economic crime cases during the first years of this period, followed by a modest decline toward the end of the period.

Indicators for white-collar crime also increased in other countries during the 1970s. The Australian Corporate Crime Commission reported a tenfold increase in cases between 1971 and 1974. In the United States, the increase in guilty verdicts against economic offenders doubled between 1972 and 1976 (Liebl 1984, pp. 26, 45).

Overall, we find a considerable increase of different indicators of economic crime in various countries. Yet these data are suited neither to confirm nor to falsify those who hypothesize a long-term increase in white-collar crime. First, the time periods are relatively short. Second, the registered increases may be due to (1) changes in institutional arrangements and (2) changing political-cultural climates.

(1) In Germany, for example, criminal justice agencies created special prosecutor's offices and court chambers for economic crime in the late 1960s and early 1970s (Kaiser 1980, p. 492). During the same period, similar steps were taken in other countries. This may well have contributed to the increase in officially recorded economic crime. At the same time, we have no information on the development of the dark figure during these years. This figure is particularly unknown in the area of white-collar crime. Banks, for example, are very reluctant to report internal computer crimes out of concern for their public reputation (Tiedemann 1976, vol. 2, p. 149). Furthermore, administrative control agencies are especially likely to observe economic offenses (Schöch 1984), but their willingness to report offenses to criminal justice agencies is often small. Their organizational interests are often better served through negotiations with deviant organizations than through long and costly court procedures (Mayntz 1983; for the German IRS see Schöch 1984).

The prosecution of economic offenses is also quite arbitrary (Berckhauer 1980). First, formal law is confusing. In Germany, economic crimes are defined in more than 200 separate federal statutes and their definition is often vague. Second, the organizational differentiation of economic crime prosecution and the considerable size and complexity of cases provide wide prosecutorial discretion despite the formal obligation to prosecute in civil law countries. Cases with damages below

100,000 German Marks are often regarded as trivial and dropped by specialized prosecutorial agencies (Berckhauer 1980, p. 230). In a random sample of 739 suspects in 407 prosecutorial procedures, the prosecution dropped charges against 469 individuals (63%) (Berckhauer 1980).

(2) Traditionally, in Germany, "white-collar crime" proved to be highly resistant to public debate. Kaiser (1980, p. 477) finds the causes for this successful resistance in the low visibility of offenses, the abstract nature of (organizational) offenders, and the highly anonymous relation between victims and offenders. While this argument is a plausible explanation for the continuous concentration of public debate on street crime as opposed to economic crime, it does not explain historical and international differences.

In the United States, Sutherland's (1940, 1945, 1949) work on white-collar crime initiated a relatively early debate on this issue. In Germany, a comparable debate emerged only thirty years later, as a bibliographic account documents (Liebl and Liebl 1985). Two explanations come to mind for this delay. First, problem generating conditions developed earlier in America: the level of economic activity, the tertiarization of the economy, and the growth of white-collar occupations.

Second, conditions for the construction of the problem, a shift in public culture and claims-making power favored an earlier debate in the United States. These factors include the long history of democratization in America and a public-political culture in which personal trust was of preeminent importance (Kalberg 1987). Democratization of German society was much delayed after the failures of the 1848 revolution and of the Weimar Republic. In addition, political practice in the reemerging (West) German democracy after World War II, partly imposed by the western powers, was initially of a rather authoritarian character. Changes in political culture emerged during the 1960s, parallel to economic growth, increasing the stability of the new democratic state and also strengthening the Social Democratic Party. These changes imply increasing mistrust of economically powerful groups in society as indicated by public opinion polls (*Allensbacher Berichte* 1983). The proportion of the population believing that entrepreneurs were inconsiderate grew from 21 percent in 1965 to 31 percent in 1976, and 39 percent in 1983 (including 48% of those 16 to 29 years). Even more people believed that entrepreneurs exploit others: 17 percent in 1965, 26 percent in 1976, and 34 percent in 1983 (including 45% of those 16 to 29 years).

Under these new structural conditions and the new cultural climate, claims against white-collar crime grew in the news media and in the legal profession—issues that have previously been discussed for America (Cullen, Maakestad, and Cavender 1987, Chapters 1 and 4; Katz 1980) and that we now discuss for the German case.

Construction of the Economic Crime Problem in the Media

Central to the construction of white-collar crime as a social problem was the increasing number and intensity of claims brought forward in the news media. We analyzed the development and structure of claims made against economic offenses in two politically influential weekly news magazines, *Die Zeit* and *Der Spiegel*.[1] Both papers are perceived by political decision makers to be liberal. They report claims that criminal justice agencies, interest groups, politicians, and others direct against economic offenders, and they produce such claims themselves. In our analysis we included the years 1960 to 1983 for *Die Zeit* and 1960 to 1984 for *Der Spiegel*.[2]

We were especially interested in two comparisons. First, which actors are presented as "typical" economic offenders and how do these images differ from those suggested by the federal criminal statistics for economic offenses? Second, how do types of norms, regulations, and sanctions demanded against white-collar offenders compare to those demanded against thievery and general property offenders?

Data and Methods of Analysis

We identified 286 articles in *Der Spiegel* and 226 in *Die Zeit* that make or report claims regarding white-collar offenses. We first measured the frequencies of articles in which such claims were made over time per magazine, and we differentiated the types of behavior challenged. In a second step we chose 202 *Die Zeit* articles (1960 to 1983) for an in-depth content analysis.[3] Units of analysis were claims contained in these articles. Since some articles made claims against different types of

1. While *Die Zeit* has the appearance of a newspaper, *Der Spiegel* has that of a magazine. Both contain reports, analyses, and commentaries on political, economic, and cultural issues. For reasons of simplicity, I use the terms magazine, paper, weekly, or newspaper for both publications throughout this text.

2. The time frame of the analysis includes as much as possible of the law-making process (1974–1986), the time of the expert commission created by the Federal Department of Justice (1972–1978), a considerable time before law-making efforts took off, and before the general political climate and the majority of the federal government changed from conservative-libertarian to social-democratic-libertarian (late 1960s).

3. This figure is lower than the total number of articles identified in *Die Zeit* (N = 226). Only those articles were selected that contain themes later to be considered in the phase of the expert commission or in the legislative process.

offenses, the number of cases (233) is higher than that of articles. The variables identified in the content analysis include: year of appearance, behavior against which claims are directed, number of lines per claim, type of offender, type of victim, type of law norm discussed, type of norm-related demand (e.g., creation, enforcement, liberalization), other claims, types of claim makers, reasons presented for justification of claims, opponents, and the latters' reasons for their opposition.

We developed these categories and what "expressions" or phenomena fell into each category inductively. Four coders collected all expressions as they appeared in the newspaper articles. We then developed more abstract or general categories under which all expressions could be subsumed unequivocally and in accordance with our theoretical interests. After several pretests and adaptations of the coding scheme, we finally coded all texts using these categorical systems. Inter-coder reliability was high after intensive coder training.

Growing Claims in the Press Against White-Collar Offenses

Articles that make claims against white-collar offenses are not equally distributed over time. Instead, claims clearly increase for both papers over the years, most remarkably during the late 1960s (see Table 1). Comparing the first two five-year periods for Die Zeit we find nearly a tripling of reports, from 10 (1960–64) to 29 (1965–69). For the next time period we find more than a twofold increase to 67 articles (1970–74). During this period the law-making process is formally initiated (late 1972). During the following two periods the number of articles remains relatively constant: 57 (1975–79), and 63 (1979–83). In Der Spiegel the number of articles starts off at a much higher level with 41 (1960–64) and 33 (1965–69) for the first time periods, increases less dramatically to 77 (1970–74), and then remains relatively constant with 63 (1975–79) and 72 (1980–84).

Purely internal changes in editorial policies may explain the more dramatic increase in one paper as compared to the other. Die Zeit is more libertarian than Der Spiegel, thus more cautious with claims against entrepreneurial behavior. Even so, the common increase in both papers, especially during the late 1960s, suggests the workings of external factors (e.g., an increase in sensational court suits or claims making in other sectors of society, the justice system, the legal sciences, politics, or public opinion).

The relative importance of editorial policy versus external factors is further clarified when we compare by magazine the development of report frequencies for specific types of offenses. While types of offenses are covered to different degrees by the two papers, relative

TABLE 1. Number of Claims-Making Articles Versus Economic Behavior over Time

Magazine	Five-year period				
	1960–64	*1965–69*	*1970–74*	*1975–79*	*1980–83/4*
Die Zeit	10	29	67	57	63 (4 years)
Der Spiegel	41	33	77	63	72
Total	51	62	144	120	135

peaks and lows appear rather abruptly and simultaneously in both papers.⁴ This suggests that the long-term coverage of specific themes is determined by the internal policies of the two papers. Yet, common peaks and lows in report frequency of individual offenses refer to external explanatory factors. Public opinion, the making of claims concerning specific offenses in the political or science sectors, and actual rates have little explanatory power as they are rather unlikely to change abruptly. Instead we have to assume that the papers pick up particularly sensational court cases—as they do in another substantive area (see Gitlin 1980). We find exemplary evidence for this assumption when the highest single year number of 25 economic crime articles in *Die Zeit* appears in 1982, the year of the "Flick affair"—a major scandal which included parts of the political sector and one of the most powerful companies in the Federal Republic of Germany, Flick. It involved tax evasion and improper contributions to political parties.

Structure of the Problem in the Press

The concentration of news media on sensational cases, as we shall see, helps to shape the image of "the" white-collar offender as a particularly powerful and high-status actor. It thereby increases the "political exchange value" (*Offe*) of white-collar crime legislation for political parties with predominantly working-class constituencies. Political exchange value is the number of votes a party can gain through a political

4. While *Der Spiegel* discusses fraud cases as early as the 1960s, *Die Zeit* picks up this theme only in the seventies. After 1970, however, we find remarkable parallels. Peaks of report frequency for both papers are the periods 1971–74, 1976–77, and 1981–82. Antitrust offenses are, until 1972, more frequently reported by Die Zeit. Once *Der Spiegel* "discovers" this theme we find common peaks (1972) and lows (1975–76, 1982) for this case too. *Die Zeit* rarely reports tax offenses. When it does, however, reports appear in the same years in which we find peaks in *Der Spiegel* (1969–70, 1976, 1980). Only reports about corruption are an exception. In *Der Spiegel*, these reports dominate in the 1960s as compared to the 1970s (18 to 4). In *Die Zeit* we find the opposite relation (0 to 12).

initiative. Concentration on sensational cases involving powerful economic actors is also welcomed by people with egalitarian values and by those who make claims against economic crime. Such reporting thus supports political initiatives for white-collar crime legislation. The structure of the problem can be understood more precisely if we consider (a) "typical" offenders and victims, (b) policy demands against white-collar crime versus street crime, and (c) who demands what against whom.

"Typical" Offenders and Victims

The 233 offenses presented describe 265 offenders. The "typical" economic offender is, according to the magazine articles, an entrepreneur, manager, or high-level executive (69.4% of all offenders mentioned). While the size of the firm or company is often unspecified, almost half of this group (34.3% of the total) are explicitly associated with big companies, much fewer with middle-sized ones (5.3%), and hardly any with small firms (0.8%). Other types of offenders are mentioned much more rarely.[5]

This distribution does not at all reflect that of defendants actually sentenced for economic offenses. Unfortunately, the categories of the federal economic crime statistics, compiled from court records, differ from the categories underlying our media analysis (Liebl 1984, pp. 128–148). Yet a very general comparison is possible. It shows that, in contrast to the high status of offenders in media stories, the power and class status of sentenced "white-collar" offenders does not differ greatly from that of all offenders in the general criminal court statistics (the one exception is a slight overrepresentation of the upper middle class among economic offenders) (Berckhauer 1980, pp. 223–224).

The distribution of the 167 victims mentioned in the magazine articles also differs from that reflected in court statistics (see Table 2). The state and the *parafisci* (semi-governmental organizations, e.g., mandatory public insurance agencies) are less frequently mentioned as victims in the newspaper (25.1%) than in the statistics (47.9%). Instead, the articles point more frequently to individual victims. These individual victims are sometimes upper-class individuals (9.6%), but most frequently relatively powerless groups such as consumers, renters, employees, immigrants, debtors, and lower-class people (35.4% in the

5. Politicians constitute 7.5 percent of reported offenders, professionals 4.9 percent, civil servants 3.8 percent, other employees 3.0 percent, real estate owners, 1.9 percent, representatives of lobby organizations 1.1 percent, and others 8.3 percent.

TABLE 2. Victims According to Media Versus Court Statistics

According to Die Zeit articles				According to court statistics	
Specific type	Percent	General category	Percent	General category	Percent
State/parafisci	25.1	State/parafisci	25.1	State/welfare organizations	47.9
Consumers	7.2	Individuals	35.4	Individuals	16.4
Renters	5.4				
Employers	4.2				
Lower classes	6.0				
Immigrants	2.4				
Bank customers	7.2				
Small debtors	3.0				
Brokers	0.6	Higher-class	9.6		
Capital investors	9.0	individuals			
Employers	0.6	Employers	0.6	Employers	3.8
Companies	11.4	Companies	27.0	Companies	23.4
Banks	11.4				
Large creditors	4.2				
Others	2.4	Others	2.4	Others	9.4

articles versus 16.4% for all individuals in the court statistics). The frequency with which the victimization of firms is reported in *Die Zeit* (27.0%) is similar to the representation of firms as victims in court statistics (23.4%).

In sum, the "truth" of the statistics and the definition of "typical" offenders and victims by the press differ considerably for the distribution of actual offenders and victims. The press presents powerful offenders and lower-class, powerless victims more frequently than do the criminal court statistics. This result remains valid if we control for the length of articles and for all time periods under consideration. Several possible explanations come to mind. First, the magazine articles are not exclusively related to criminalized behavior. For example, they may make claims against antitrust offenses which are merely administrative offenses in the FRG. Second, the press concentrates on the most sensational cases which, in cases of economic crime, typically involve more powerful offenders. Finally, class bias in the implementation of criminal law may contribute to the gap between the presentation of reality in the press and in the reality of criminal courts. Further investigations are needed to evaluate and test these hypotheses and to determine the relative explanatory power of the different factors.

Policy Demands Against White-Collar Crime Versus Street Crime

Ninety explicit demands for policy changes were expressed for 76 cases discussed in *Die Zeit*. These cases are of particular interest for our analysis since they contribute more of an atmosphere for legal change than general claims.

Most demands aim at tougher criminal law provisions (23.3%) and at the passing of new ones (15%). Others concern stricter enforcement of existing norms (13.3%), additional resources for the criminal justice system (6.7%), a specification of criminal law provisions (8.9%), or the prevention of offenses through new civil (15.6%) and noncriminal public law norms (5.6%). We find few demands for more *lenient* criminal law (3.3%), more flexibility for the criminal justice system (2.2%), victim-offender compensation (1.1%), or more research to enhance the understanding of white-collar crime (2.2%).

In sum, *Die Zeit*, a newspaper known for its libertarian orientation in the field of criminal justice, poses or reports predominantly punitive demands (58.3%) against white-collar offenders. Two-thirds of these demands are directed at the legislature and one-third at criminal justice agencies.

How does this orientation relate to patterns of demand for action regarding non-white-collar offenses? Our findings can be usefully compared with others on newspaper claims concerning theft and general property offenses, that is, offenses typically committed by lower-class offenders (see Table 3). Haferkamp (1980) analyzed 148 normative demands regarding these offenses identified in two daily newspapers, the *Frankfurter Allgemeine Zeitung (FAZ)* and the *Frankfurter Rundschau (FR)*, covering the years 1961 to 1976. Yet, Haferkamp identified only 36 percent of all demands in *FAZ* and in *FR* as punitive, compared to 58.3 percent punitive demands on white-collar issues in *Die Zeit*. New and sharper criminal law norms are demanded in only 10 percent of his cases, but in 38.3 percent of ours. Several plausible explanations for this difference in punitiveness must be dismissed. The general ideological orientation of the newspapers cannot account for the more punitive orientation identified in our analysis. While *Die Zeit* is liberal, Haferkamp's analysis includes both a liberal (*FR*) and a conservative paper (*FAZ*). It also cannot be argued that Haferkamp's analysis included a more liberal time period than ours. Taking years common to both studies (1961–1974), *Die Zeit* still shows an average of 50 percent punitive demands. It is thus likely that the type of offense explains the difference in demands. Demands against powerful and high-status offenders are more punitive than demands against lower- and middle-class property offenders, at least in West Germany of the 1960s and 1970s.

TABLE 3. Types of Offenses by Punitiveness of Demands (Percents)

	Types of offenses	
Types of demands	White-collar offenses	General property offenses
Demands for new criminal code provisions	38.3	10
Demands for sharper implementation of existing criminal provisions	20.0	26.0
Nonpunitive demands	41.7	64.0

Who Demands What Against Whom?

Who poses these punitive demands and against which offender groups are they directed? We identified 141 demanders for 94 of the cases (see Table 4). While we cannot determine to what degree the distributions reflect bias of the press or actual representations of demand patterns of the groups cited, the following picture is presented.

Political parties are rarely cited as demanders. In only two cases do the conservatives (Christian-Democrats) want stricter norms against employees to protect state and companies from victimization. The Social Democrats demand stricter or more precise norms in three cases. Here, firms are identified as offenders and consumers as victims. This party specific distribution reflects the clientele-oriented sanctioning patterns of political parties we identified for the legislative process (see Chapter 4.).

Associations and lobby organizations present a differentiated picture. The articles typically cite specialized interest groups with rather punitive demands against very specific offenses. The more specific and homogeneous these groups' purposes, memberships, and "hostile" environments are, the more specific and punitive are their demands. Consumer and tenant organizations are reported with three punitive demands. They point to offenses that hurt their members and clienteles and to offender groups whose interest is opposed to their own.

Labor unions, on the other hand, pose three punitive demands involving a variety of victims. This reflects the relatively broad engagement of modern German unions in housing construction, capital investment, and banking as well as in the representation of labor interests.

Our findings were counterintuitive for industry and employers' associations. Seven of their 16 demands were punitive and directed against companies, firms, and industry in general. This is in sharp contrast to findings from the law-making process, where industry associations

TABLE 4. Types of Demand by Claims Makers in *Die Zeit* Articles

Claims maker	Percent of all demands	Demands in absolute numbers		
		Sharper norms or implementation	Specification of criminal provisions and non-criminal law	Other
CDU/CSU	1.5	2	0	0
SPD	2.2	2	1	0
FDP	1.5	0	1	1
Parliament	2.2	0	2	1
Executive branch	12.5	12	3	2
Specific departments				
Justice	2.2	2	1	0
Economics	2.2	2	1	0
Budget	5.1	2	5	0
Prosecutors	6.6	6	2	1
Judges	3.7	4	1	0
Police	1.5	2	0	0
Trust Control Administration	8.8	7	5	0
IRS	2.2	3	0	0
Other public admin.	2.2	2	1	0
Associations				
Industry	11.0	7	7	2
Consumer	1.5	1	0	1
Labor	2.2	3	0	0
Tenant	2.2	3	0	0
Other	2.2	2	1	0
Journalists	14.7	12	6	1
Academics	5.1	4	3	0
Others	6.6			

appeared as important lobby groups fighting the criminalization of their clienteles. The main reason for their seemingly self-accusing behavior in the press may be the internal differentiation of the economy. Demands are often directed against other economic sectors. And indeed, companies are often victims of economic offenses committed by and in other firms (e.g., suppliers). One potential explanation is that before concrete legislative or judicial steps are initiated, public demands do not obligate companies actually to support punitive policies. Another possible factor may be that industry associations, who wish to avoid tainting their reputation, have reason to distance themselves from offenders when scandals occur.

Criminal justice agencies were much less represented among the cited claims makers (11.8%, N = 16) than previous research suggests for the American case (e.g., Hagan 1980). This lack of participation in the media is not too surprising, however, considering the high influence of criminal justice agencies in the concrete law-making process (see below). These agencies depend much less than other groups on public and indirect ways of influencing criminal justice-related political decision making. The relatively few demands from criminal justice agencies were mostly punitive (12 of 16), but not more so than the average of all demands. Police and prosecutors plead for a strengthening of their agencies and for more effective investigation (8 of 11), while judges plead for stricter legal provisions and for more justice (4 of 5 demands).

Journalists of *Die Zeit* posed 14.7 percent of all demands without reference to any interest group. The distribution of offender and victim categories in these cases is similar to that discussed by other groups. Journalists justify their demands with the same arguments as other groups. There are two ways to interpret this finding: either as support for the thesis that mass media are merely distributors of public knowledge rather than independent actors in claims making against deviant behavior; or as support for the competing thesis that journalists select cases so as to support their own views and thereby construct a reality that differs from that of all other actors as well as from the reality of statistics.

Finally, how are the main types of demand distributed over the different types of offenders and victims? The disproportionate representation of high status and powerful actors among the offender groups is not repeated when demands are posed against particular groups. In fact, 60 percent of claims directed against employees request new and more punitive provisions. Employees are followed by civil servants, professionals, and real estate owners. Fifty percent of all demands directed against these groups are punitive. Entrepreneurs, managers, and high-level executives are only the next group subjected to punitive demands. Within this group, however, the old pattern of stricter demands against the more powerful is repeated, with 34.4 percent of demands against big companies, 20 percent against medium-sized firms, and no demands against small firms.

With regard to victims we find that the powerlessness of victims correlates with the punitiveness of demands against the offenders. When small lenders and foreign immigrant workers are victimized, all demands are punitive. The proportion of punitive demands is 87.9 percent when employees are victims. The smallest proportion of punitive demands target offenders against companies and firms (42.9%). Only two cases depart from the pattern that concentrates punitive demands on offenders against powerless victims. When consumers and capital investors are victimized, the proportion of punitive demands is 44.4 percent and 75 percent respectively.

Selection Bias of the Press and Public Opinion

The selection bias of press reporting is considerable compared to that of the criminal justice system. In general, the media focus on powerful and high-status offenders and favor using the criminal law to protect the powerless. The media are also more likely to demand the criminal punishment of economic offenders than of general offenders.

During the time period under consideration, and parallel to claims making against powerful and high-status economic actors, we find growing negative public opinion about entrepreneurs. As noted previously, social surveys show that the percentage of people who believe entrepreneurs are inconsiderate and exploit others increased during the 1960s and 1970s. The idea that entrepreneurs run "dirty businesses" and that they lack consciences also increased during the same years. While this belief was shared by 10 percent of the general population in 1965, it increased to 17 percent in 1976 and to 25 percent in 1983 (including 31% of the 16–19 year olds) (see Allensbacher Berichte 1983).

These data do not resolve the longstanding debate on whether the media are more a reflection or a producer of public opinion. Yet the patterns of claims making we have identified suggest that the press did *at least* function to reinforce public opinion. It probably also popularized the image in the minds of political decision makers that economic crimes were committed by powerful offenders who preyed on weak and vulnerable victims. And it may very well have informed political decision makers that initiatives against white-collar offenders were politically attractive.

Construction of Economic Crime and the Legal Profession

The legal profession and actors of the criminal justice system had not played any noteworthy role in public media claims making against economic crime. Yet the legal profession did become prominently involved in the emerging political debate in 1972, when the issue of economic crime became the main theme of the criminal law division of the 49th Meeting of the German Lawyers Association (*Verein Deutscher Juristentag*). More specifically, the question to be debated was: "What criminal justice strategies are best suited to fight economic crime effectively?" The timing of this debate was significant. The Federal Department of Justice had just decided to establish an expert commission for the fight against economic crime (*Sachverständigenkommission zur Bekämpfung der Wirtschaftskriminalität—Reform des Wirtschaftsstrafrechts*). Klaus Tiedemann, a prominent professor of criminal law and criminology, presented an extensive expert opinion for the Lawyers Association. The meetings were opened on September 19, 1972, by presentations from a prominent police chief, Dr. Herbert Schäfer and a renowned scholar of criminal law, Professor Peter Noll. Both speakers presented a list of normative theses or recommendations directed at the federal government. These theses were discussed during the following two days and then voted on in plenary sessions. Between 200 and 500 people attended the lectures and debates, with almost fifty lawyers actively contributing. The number of voting participants varied between 145 and 85.[6]

All participants at the meetings were members of the legal profession. Their participation in the debate on antitrust issues varied with their occupation. The largest number of the 97 contributions to the debate were from lawyers employed by federal and state justice departments (28 contributors), followed by criminal jurisprudents (23) and prosecutors (18). All other groups were less involved: defense attorneys (10), judges (8), members of the trust control administration (3), business organizations (2), and others (5).

The debate was chaired by the previous chief prosecutor of the State of Bremen, Hans Dünnebier, a person with considerable experience on government commissions. Four types of demands were discussed and voted on. First, most of the requests for intensive research on economic crime passed. Second, demands for more effective organization and more generous funding of those criminal justice agencies that specialize in economic crime were also supported by the majority of participants. Third, demands for a redefinition of (economic) administrative offenses into criminal offenses and of misdemeanor (noneconomic) crimes into administrative offenses were supported in some cases but not in others. Fourth, demands for a weakening of due process rights in economic crime cases were rejected.

More specifically, the debate was organized by ten topic areas. Theses put forth by Schäfer and Noll on each of these topics were discussed and voted on.

1. A strong majority voted for the introduction of federal statistics on economic crime. A majority also voted for Noll's demand to

---

6. While all lawyers are allowed to participate in the meetings of the German Lawyers Association, only its members have voting rights.

decriminalize several types of common misdemeanor crimes for the sake of additional criminal justice resources to fight economic offenses.

2. Demands to provide more resources for more intense educational preparation of police, prosecutors, and judges for the fight against economic crime also achieved clear majorities.

3. It was further voted that federal and state governments create a central institute for applied criminological research (*Kriminologische Zentralstelle*) which should advise the government in the promulgation of laws against economic crime. Business associations were asked to promote research in this area.

4. Other proposals faced severe opposition in the debate and were voted down. One example was the demand to strengthen the position of victims in criminal justice procedures against economic crime. Proposals to speed up the adjudication of economic cases were considerably modified and cut back before they were passed in more moderate terms. It was requested that the legal requirement be removed to read all documents used as evidence in trials. In addition, participants supported the demand that lay judges, selected in economic crime cases, ought to have particular expertise in business issues.

5. The participants strongly refuted the request to weaken banking and tax secrecy in criminal justice investigations. They also voted down the request that all administrative agencies ought to inform prosecutors' offices about any economic offenses they detect in the course of their administrative obligations. Another demand to grant investigators access to documents that economic crime suspects had deposited with their attorneys was first passed but later withdrawn after heavy protests by defense attorneys.

6. The sixth area of discussion concerned issues of the criminal liability of corporations and their employees. These issues, later to become central in the legislative process, were heavily disputed at this stage. The demand to collect criminal fines from business organizations that had been engaged in corporate crime was rejected. Slight majorities were achieved for two related options: first, to criminalize negligent supervisors if their negligence contributed to criminal behavior (*Aufsichtspflichtverletzung*); second, to criminalize those individuals who had engaged in criminal activities on behalf of their organization (*Vertreterhaftung*).

7. A majority voted to consider the amount of damage caused in assessing a crime's seriousness. Strongly rejected, however, was the suggestion to shift the burden of proof to the defendant in economic crime cases.

8. Another item that later became central in the legislative process, the criminalization of antitrust offenses, was also debated. Representatives of industry associations raised considerable concerns. In his theses, Noll had demanded distinguishing between criminal and administrative offenses on the basis of quantitative criteria, that is, the amount of damage caused. This would have upgraded most antitrust violations from administrative to criminal offenses. Noll withdrew this demand after severe criticism in the course of the deliberations. Yet a proposal by criminal law professor Grünewald to upgrade administrative to criminal offenses on the basis of the criterion of wrongfulness (*Unrechtsgehalt*) passed with a clear majority. Speakers of economic lobbying organizations unsuccessfully attempted to exclude antitrust offenses from this proposal. They were, however, successful in their opposition against the demand to publicize administrative antitrust offenses and to establish a public register of economic repeat offenders. These proposals were rejected.

9. The next set of issues dealt with limitations of entrepreneurial liberties for the sake of crime prevention. Three such proposals passed: to extend bookkeeping obligations; to increase the publicity of selected business transactions; and to tighten the conditions for the incorporation of organizations with limited liability status.

10. Finally, the assembly discussed the creation of research institutions exclusively devoted to issues of white-collar crime. Schäfer's demand for a research institute for economic crime law was rejected. Instead, the majority pleaded for the creation of a government commission with inquisitorial power and privileged access to banking and tax information.

While it is not possible to explain the agenda or the decision-making patterns presented here, we can propose some hypotheses. The positive vote for increased criminal justice resources and further specialization is a function of the legal profession's interest in furthering its career avenues and professionalization. Likewise, increased research on issues of white-collar crime will increase the resources available to the very agencies, practitioners, and scholars involved in these discussions and can thus be easily explained.

Discussions and votes on proposals to weaken due process rights of the accused and defendants in economic cases took a markedly different course. Such theses had been primarily presented by Noll and had been supported by other legal scholars. In the light of Weber's concept of substantive rationalization, they are attempts to weaken and reduce formal rights of powerful defendants, as compared to rights of common criminals, and thereby to establish greater substantive equality between different social classes in the criminal justice system. Yet the vast majority of lawyers rejected such endeavors for the sake of formal legal rights. They ranked the rule of law and principles of legal order higher than ideas of substantive equality. This opposition was manifested by both defense attorneys and prosecutors. Members from the Federal Department of Justice fought especially hard to preserve rights that had only recently been fortified in the major liberalizing criminal law reform of the 1960s.

The Emerging Intervention of Industry Associations
by Peter Brühl

Industry and business associations had taken great interest in the meetings of the Lawyers Association. The rise of economic crime issues, increasing public claims against entrepreneurs, the establishment of a government commission, and the topic of the meetings had alarmed their leaders. On May 29, 1972 the chair of the division for antitrust policies of the German Federation of Industry (*Bund der Deutschen Industrie*, BDI) sent a letter to members of the Federation's working group and committee on antitrust law. In this letter, he announced that extensive debate on antitrust offenses was likely to be held at the Lawyers Association meetings. He encouraged members to attend the meetings and to participate in its deliberations and votes. According to interview information, the *BDI* division for legal affairs also encouraged its committee members to participate. In a letter dated October 3, 1972, the chair of the Federation's antitrust division reported on a meeting and "thorough conversations" among himself, members of the antitrust committee, representatives of the Association of Chemical Industry, and Professor Tiedemann (the lawyer in charge of the expert opinion for the Lawyers Association meetings).

Some of the industry lawyers did indeed participate in the Lawyers Association deliberations on economic crime. As expected, antitrust offenses became a central issue. Already in his introductory lecture, Professor Noll refered to antitrust offenses as an example for "many types of behavior . . . in which the law defines truly criminal forms of behavior as administrative offenses and thereby reaffirms offenders of the negligible quality of these offenses" (*Verhandlungen des 49. DJT*, M 21). He presented his normative thesis # 11, according to which the distinction between criminal and administrative offenses should follow quantitative criteria only (ibid., M 200). This would have redefined most antitrust offenses from administrative to criminal. Noll also suggested, in his thesis, # 12d, that a publicly accessible file be established in which "especially dangerous economic offenders" with a prior white-collar crime record should be registered (ibid., M 200). These theses were partially supported by Professor Lüderssen, another renowned scholar of criminal jurisprudence (ibid., M 124f, M 155).

Ten additional persons participated in this debate, among them Dr. Benisch, a lawyer from BDI, and Dr. Sünner, a representative of BASF, a powerful chemical corporation. Dr. Benisch argued that, in international comparison, sanctions against antitrust offenses were already particularly severe, well publicized, and effective. Concurring with the Vice President of the Federal Trust Control Administration (*Bundeskartellamt*), he expressed considerable doubts about the feasibility of distinguishing between administrative and criminal offenses on the basis of quantitative criteria (ibid., M 137f). Following additional criticism, Noll withdrew this request while a related proposal by Professor Grünewald (Bonn University), was passed "with an overwhelming majority," as noted above (ibid., M 155). This proposal suggested that "offenses with a high degree of blameworthiness" (ibid., M 154), should be recategorized from administrative to criminal.

Lüderssen's suggestion to publicize administrative fines was supported by the Vice President of the Federal Trust-Control Administration, and by Mr. Groß, a lawyer from the Hesse Department of Justice. Their arguments, however, were successfully challenged by Dr. Benisch, the antitrust specialist of the BDI, and the thesis was voted down (ibid., M 155). A similar proposal by Noll was defeated after the intervention by "a lawyer" (ibid., M 156f, M 162), and speakers for the North Rhine-Westphalian and Federal Departments of Justice (ibid., M 164f, M 166f) (ibid., M 169).

After the meetings, the relevant BDI divisions evaluated the results and drew conclusions for future strategies in letters from September 28 and October 3, 1972. While the antitrust division simply described the course of deliberations, the legal affairs division also commented on the participation: "Some problematic proposals of Professor Noll did find a majority of the vote. This is partly due to the fact that, despite our request, only relatively few corporate lawyers participated in the meetings. They were clearly outnumbered by judges, prosecutors, and ministerial bureaucrats. . . . In another case [voted barely in favor of industry's interests] a better vote could have been achieved."

In sum, the German Industry Federation had taken two steps with regard to the 49th Meeting of the Lawyers Association. First, a meeting was arranged with Professor Tiedemann, the author of the basic opinion for the Lawyers Association. While Tiedemann's report had already been written and could no longer be influenced, this meeting served to inform Federation members about the directions the deliberations might take. Second, the Federation encouraged members of industry associations and corporations to participate and vote at the meetings. While any lawyer is allowed to participate in the meetings, only members of the Lawyers Association have voting rights. Sudden waves of new memberships shortly before meetings often indicate that associations consider issues important and mobilize their lawyers (Redeker 1978). For example, the German Employers Association (*Deutscher Arbeitgeberverband*) mobilized hundreds of lawyers to join the Lawyers Association when central issues of labor law were scheduled for the 52nd Meeting in 1978. All proposals during these latter meetings were decided in the interest of the Employers Association.

The Industry Federation did not succeed in mobilizing a similar movement against the criminalization of antitrust offenses. Obviously members had not perceived their interests to be sufficiently concerned. Most members may have perceived that only marginal groups within industry would be affected by the criminalization of antitrust offenses. Yet, limited mobilization had occurred, speakers of the German Industry Federation and related organizations did take the floor, and some anti-industry proposals were successfully defeated. The industrial anti-criminalization front had begun to emerge.

Chapter 4
The Expert Commission: Developing the Claims and First Resistance

Researchers have increasingly discussed the roles of scholars and practitioners as participants in criminal law-making processes. Such experts played a major role in the promulgation of criminal law norms against white-collar crime in the FRG. This chapter examines how their participation influenced the rationales of decision makers.

When one wants to learn about different types of consulting processes and their effects on political decision making, the following questions need to be asked. Who selects what kind of consultants? What is the degree of rationality and what are the rationales of these consultants? What are the dynamics and networks in such consulting processes, within an expert commission and between consultants and decision makers? Which experts and which scientific rationality finally influence political decision-making processes? How important are they in decision makers' political rationalities, and how do decision makers evaluate experts and scientific rationality against power potentials and the interests of important lobbying groups?

We address these questions by analyzing documents from the law-making process. We also conducted interviews with most members of the former expert commission that prepared these and other law norms for the prevention and sanctioning of economic crime. At the outset, we report some findings from the literature and relate this issue of experts to our theoretical concerns.

Theoretical Considerations: Experts, Knowledge, and Rationality

Concerned with the rationality and substantive rationales that experts contribute to the political process, we refer to rationality in two distinct ways. First, we mean purposive rationality (*Zweckrationalität*), as defined by Max Weber (see Weber 1976, p. 12), that is, the degree to which different means were compared in terms of their expected goal achievement and other desired or undesired consequences. Second, we investigate substantive rationalities. Certain means are rational only with regard to particular purposes or values. What is rational in terms of economic policy may not be rational in terms of legal or criminal policies and vice versa (see Chapter 2).

In this context Weber's prognosis of an increasing intrusion of socio-logical, economic, and other reasoning into formal legal discourse is especially crucial. Formal rationality is concerned with the guarantee of liberty in terms of the libertarian bourgeois state. It was the ground on which free exchange could grow in a society no longer integrated by normative consensus. Substantive rationality, on the other hand, may relate to liberty in a sociological sense, that is, to the actual (not just formal) chances of people to choose and act freely. Substantive rationality may alternatively relate to other criteria such as economic growth, technological progress, or the protection of particular corporations.

For emerging welfare states Weber expects substantive intrusions upon the formal rationality of the legal system, and the partial replacement of legal norms by sociological, economic, and ethical reasoning (see Chapter 2). Weber's conclusion that this substantive intrusion upon the legal system means a loss of specific legal rationality has experienced considerable criticism. In particular, representatives of the Habermas school have argued that there have always been substantive standards in what Weber considered value-neutral formal legal terms (e.g., freedom of contract) (Eder 1978; see also Trubek 1985, 1986). According to this school, recent legal change does not imply substantivation of law but rather the explication of substantive elements which had always been present in formal law. Through explication these substantive elements become available to rational discourse. What Weber interprets as substantivation and as the cause for a loss of rationality, Eder interprets as an explication of immanent substantive standards and thus as the basis for a "real" rationalization of law.

Following Kohlberg's concept of the post-conventional level of societal development, Eder argues that the making and application of law in post-modern societies are increasingly based on the rational agreement of all participants in the legal process. Such law would eventually be truely based on the ethics of responsibility (*Verantwortungsethik*)[1] and serve the interests of all members of society. While we disagree with

---

1. Weber's term, *Verantwortungsethik*, refers to an ethic that takes the consequences of acting into account, as opposed to *Gesinnungsethik*, which refers only to the value of the action in itself.

Eder's underlying philosophical idea that a rational agreement on different interests and values is possible, his thoughts about the recent explication of the implicit substantive aspects of formal law are relevant for this analysis (Schluchter 1981). The substantivation of law, as assumed by Weber, and the explication of implicit substantive aspects, as assumed by Eder, both have consequences for rationality and for the role of scientific experts in legal systems and processes. Neither necessarily excludes the other. To the contrary, both assume the increasing relevance of economic, sociological, and ethical reasoning in law. Their implications for the rationality of law differ. Here Weber is far from sharing Eder's utopian views on the basis of epistemological, theoretical, and empirical grounds. Weber's position is supported where neo-Marxist arguments are directed against the utopian view of the Habermas school that Eder represents (see Breuer 1977). This analysis is an attempt to examine both the common and contradictory hypotheses and predictions of Weber and Eder.

Whose rationales and modes of thinking have access to law-making processes? There is some agreement among a diversity of authors who conducted empirical research on the German and Austrian cases. There is no doubt among legal sociologists and criminologists about the central role of the legal profession in the making of criminal law. Blankenburg and Treiber (1975) find that lawyers dominate in law-making processes in general. Schick (1983) shows that almost all actors in the reform of the Austrian criminal code were lawyers. The only exception are physicians who gave testimony on the abortion issue. This primacy of the legal profession does not necessarily have positive implications for jurisprudence, but it certainly has negative consequences for empirical disciplines such as institutional economics, political science, and sociology. Schick finds that empirically oriented criminologists were not involved in the criminal code reform at all. Analyzing the effects of a variety of applied and empirical studies in legal sociology, Gessner (1984) similarly finds little openness within the German legal profession to sociological thinking. He concludes that interests of legal policy makers in the social sciences are highly selective.

The relevance of jurisprudence for criminal law making is also disputed. Martin Schubarth (1980), a legal scholar, investigates the making of three criminal law norms. He finds that practitioners of law have a much higher weight in decision making than jurisprudents. According to Schubarth, this is due to a strictly dogmatic rather than empirical or policy orientation of German criminal jurisprudence. This highly dogmatic orientation is caused by the examination system of the universities, the career criteria of legal scholars, and the orientation of legislators. Legislators are more interested in votes and in satisfying the criminal justice system than in results from empirical legal research, which is mostly used for legitimatory purposes.

In sum, German jurisprudents and sociologists generally agree on the primacy of the legal profession in criminal law making, and most authors see little or no chance for the empirical sciences to play a role in the process. This, of course, would have significant consequences, particularly considering Weber's (and Eder's) arguments about the intrusion (or explication) of substantive, economic, sociological, and ethical reasoning upon or in legal discourse. These consequences are a primacy of dogmatic jurisprudence over legal realism, a lack of purposive rationality despite a rhetorical stress of policy purposes, and instead the consideration of political opportunities and of professional group interests within criminal justice in criminal law making.[2]

The implications of such findings for the political and legislative process are far from the rational and consensual utopia of the Habermas school. They support Weber's concerns that, despite the intentions of its promoters, substantivation may contribute to a loss of legal rationality altogether and to new problems of social justice (Weber 1978, pp. 886–887 and 892–893). Some policy makers share these concerns. Schoreit (1974), a lawyer from the Federal Department of Justice, sees criminal policy as dominated by "transcendental" demands instead of being rationally oriented toward crime reduction and empirical reality. And scholars agree. Seidel (1980) identifies a high degree of terminological imprecision and contradictory use of language in his analysis of the parliamentary debates on criminal law reform. Schick (1983) argues that common sense assumptions of law makers rather than empirical knowledge determine criminal law making. He identifies such assumptions as a function of public opinion and as immediate reflections of value convictions.

Experts in the Law-Making Process: Structure and Dynamics of Participation

We analyzed documents from the law-making process, and conducted intensive interviews with twelve of the seventeen actors who had served as members of the expert commission throughout its existence. We first

---

2. Kassebaum and Ward (1991) make a similar point for the American debate on the rehabilitation of criminal offenders. Stryker (1989, 1990a), on the other hand, discusses the growing consideration of substantive rationales in the United States, for which she uses the term "technocratization" (for limits to technocratization see Stryker 1989, 1990b). It is likely that the contrast between the considerable weight Stryker finds for technocratic expertise in American law and the situation described here is due more to the regulatory areas she is concerned with (especially labor relations) than to the differ-

present a causal model that our analysis then follows. We analyze structures and dynamics within the expert commission, and cognitive structures of members of the commission. Later we show how the commission's work is or is not reflected in the arguments of political decision makers in the judicial committee of the *Bundestag*. We then draw preliminary conclusions about (1) the access of different types of experts to consulting transactions at different stages of the law-making process; (2) the rationalities, the knowledge, and the cognitions that different experts contributed; and (3) the specific weight the experts' voices had among the other experts.

The role of experts and scientists must be specified for each phase in the history of the law-making process. Their involvement took concrete forms when claims making in news media had reached its peak. We have already discussed how, in 1972, economic crime was the main topic at the meetings of the Lawyers Association. This event coincided with a thorough expert opinion on the state of economic crime written for the Federal Department of Justice by Klaus Tiedemann, now professor of criminal law and criminology from the University of Freiburg Law School. Finally, the Justice Department initiated an expert commission on this topic.

The expert commission, on which much of this analysis concentrates, was asked to consider adequate measures for the reduction of economic crime. This commission met for fifteen separate week-long meetings between 1972 and 1978. It formulated a comprehensive catalogue with suggestions for additions to and modifications of criminal and economic law (Bundesminister der Justiz 1980), and submitted them to the Department of Justice. Based on these suggestions, the Department of Justice developed two bills, including one for the Second Law Against Economic Crime.

Empirical Materials, Methods, and the Causal Model

Materials analyzed to study the role of experts include documents from the work of the expert commission and from a hearing held by the Judicial Committee of the *Bundestag*. The Department of Justice published fifteen volumes on the expert commission—one each for the week-long meetings. Each volume contains summary minutes, reporting the results of the votes on each suggestion, and the expert opinions and papers that were presented. Since these minutes do not reflect the

---

ence in national context. Criminal law making may always and everywhere be driven more by symbolic politics and interests of the staff than by instrumental rationality (see also Sutton 1988; Chapter 8).

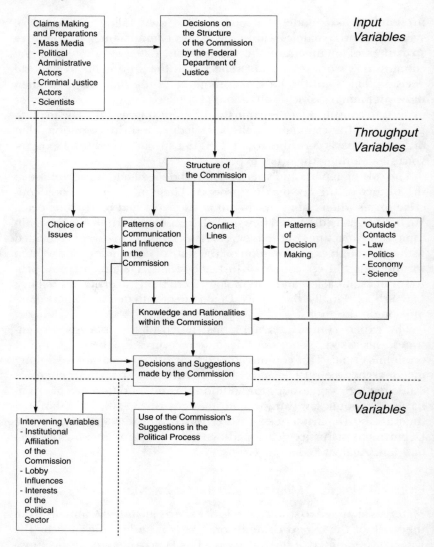

Figure 2. The causal model: role of the expert commission in the law-making process.

informal structures and dynamics of the commission, we conducted interviews, lasting from one to two hours, with twelve of the fifteen members of the commission who regularly participated. We then ana-lyzed the transcripts of these interviews. The analysis of the hearing is based on the minutes and on observations by two researchers.

The open questionnaire for the interviews was structured according to the causal model presented in Figure 2. We asked questions on each of its variables and causal relations. The causal model is structured according to four types of variables or sections of the causal process: input, throughput, intervening, and outcome variables.

The input variables deal with factors that contributed to the composition of the expert commission and to the choice of issues the commission discussed. Here two groups of factors were particularly important: (1) preceding claims made in the public, by mass media, actors from the political-administrative system, and scientists; and (2) the type of actors and institution that decided on the composition of the commission.

Within the group of throughput variables, the composition of the commission is of strategic importance. This composition influences the choice of issues deemed relevant. The first selection of issues for further consideration after the claims-making phase occurred at this point by deciding which topics would reach the next level of the definition of the social problem and which others would be left to the field of non-decision making. Other factors determined by the composition of the commission include: the influence structure, conflict lines, and decision-making patterns within the commission; relevant contacts to specific "outside worlds" in the spheres of the economy, politics, law, and science; and finally the "knowledge" (degree of rationality and types of rationalities) that became relevant in and available to the commission. This last factor depended, of course, on which carriers of knowledge were present in the commission, the communication chances different actors had within the commission, and the "windows" that existed to the "outside world." Knowledge, rationality, and rationalities, in combination with other intervening variables, determined the decisions and suggestions made by the commission and then passed on into the political process.

The use of knowledge, rationality, and rationalities in the political process depended on several intervening factors: the institutional affiliation of the commission with the criminal justice section of the Department of Justice, influences of lobbying groups, and political interests of actors in the political sector.

The following presentation of the empirical material follows the flow of this theoretical model. The hypotheses contained in the causal model can be illustrated and specified. In this chapter, we concentrate on the throughput variables. Structural and dynamic factors, discussed in the first section, are analyzed mostly on the basis of the interview materials. The following section deals with the rationalities of the commission members' arguments, applying the cognitive mapping approach to their contributions on central issues of the 1982 proposal of the Second Law Against Economic Crime. These cognitive structures are compared with those of experts in a later stage of the law-making process, the hearing organized by the judicial committee during the parliamentary phase. Finally, we show how these rationalities are or are not used in the political sector by analyzing the cognitive maps of the members of the judicial committee based on their discussions of these same topics.

Experts: Structures and Dynamics

Three crucial questions must be addressed at this point of the discussion. What kind of experts from which social spheres have access to the consulting process? Who became a member of the core group of consultants, the expert commission? And, who had the say within this group?

Table 5 gives an overview of the types of experts, according to different social spheres, who were involved in the law-making process. For the expert commission, it differentiates between permanent members and invited experts who had been asked by the commission to contribute to specific topics. For the hearing, it distinguishes among experts according to the issues on which they testified.

The economy—that is, members of firms and economic lobbying organizations—is hardly represented in the stage of the expert commission (4.2% of all participants in this phase, i.e., all persons listed in the first two columns of Table 5). Yet the economy is well represented at the hearing, forming nearly one-third of the experts (32% of all participants in this phase, i.e., all persons listed in the third through fifth columns). Within the economic sector, capital was much more represented than unions or consumer organizations.

The social control sector was heavily represented in both phases, with more than one-third of the experts in the commission phase (35%), and with more than half at the hearing. In the context of the commission almost all of these participants worked in the criminal justice system, and most were prosecutors. At the hearing two-thirds of the control agents were from the criminal justice system, police and prosecutors in equal proportions. The remaining one-third represented other control agencies, particularly the trust-control administration.

The political-administrative sector was represented in the phase of the commission with almost one-third of the participants (29.4%). Most of these were members of federal and state ministries who specialized on related issues. At the hearing, by definition, no political agent was heard.

The science sector contributed one-third of the participants in the commission phase (32.2%), and approximately one-sixth of those at the hearing (16%). During the commission phase, slightly over half the science participants were professors for economic law, trade law, or other related fields of civil law. About one-third were professors for criminal law; only four invited speakers (less than one-fifth) represented other fields: two professors for business administration, one for public law, and one criminologist. Four scholars spoke at the hearing: one criminal lawyer, one economic lawyer, one economist, and one criminologist.

With the increasing politicization of the decision-making process as it moved from the expert commission to the parliamentary hearings, experts representing lobbying groups apparently gained in their involvement. The representation of economic groups in the parliamentary phase, despite their exclusion in the commission phase, is particularly remarkable.[3] While the science sector was clearly present in both phases, its representation diminished in the parliamentary phase. Almost all scholars were jurisprudents of economic or criminal law. The economic sciences were barely represented, and the social sciences not at all. Participants in the commission phase were recruited one-third each from the social control sector, the political-administrative sector, and the science sector.

The members of the expert commission constitute the core group among all experts. They decided on the topics addressed, invested the most consulting work (fifteen week-long meetings plus preparation), and formulated and voted on the suggestions finally made to the law makers. It is worthwhile, therefore, to take a closer look at the composition of this group. Its members were chosen by the Federal Department of Justice, specifically by the head of its criminal law section. In some cases persons were approached, in others specific organizations were asked to nominate members. All members of the commission were chosen as individuals and were not representatives of their organizations.

Table 6 gives an overview of the commission members, their professional groups or organizations, the regularity of their participation in the commission, their educational background, their position during their membership, and their professional career. Those members with whom an interview was conducted are also indicated.

Two members of the commission were drawn from the criminal law sections of two state justice departments: member A from Social Dem-

3. Industry federation documents confirm that there was relatively little contact between experts and industry during the commission phase.

TABLE 5. Number of Experts in the Law-Making Process by Societal Sector

Societal spheres			Expert commission		Experts with the hearing of the Bundestag Judicial Committee			
			Members	Invited experts	Price fixing	Computer crime	Lending of "illegal" workers	Totals
Economy (3/8) (4.2%/32%)	Capital (2/7) (2.8%/28%)	Industry organizations	0	2 (3.8%)	2	2	1	5 (20%)
		Firms	0	0	0	2	0	2 (8%)
	Employees, consumers (1/1) (1.4%/4%)	Unions, consumer organizations	0	1	0	0	1	1 (4%)
Social control (24/13) (35%/52%)	Criminal justice system (21/9) (30.8%/36%)	Police	2 (11%)	0	1	1	3	5 (20%)
		State attorneys	4 (22%)	5 (9.5%)	2	0	2	4 (16%)
		Courts	1 (5.5%)	4 (7.4%)	0	0	0	0
		Defense attorneys	1 (5.5%)	4 (7.4%)	0	0	0	0
	Other agencies (3/4) (4.2%/16%)	Trust control administrations	0	1 (1.9%)	2	0	0	2 (8%)
		Other	1 (5.5%)	1 (1.9%)	0	0	1	2 (8%)

	Politics (21/0) (29.4%/0%)			Academia (23/4) (32.2%/16%)		
Ministries	2 (11%)	16 (30.4%)	0	0	0	0
Political parties	3 (16.5%)	0	0	0	0	0
Criminal law	1 (5.5%)	6 (11.4%)	0	1	0	1 (4%)
Economic law	3 (16.5%)	9 (17.1%)	1	0	0	1 (4%)
Economics	0	2 (3.8%)	1	0	0	1 (4%)
Criminology	0	1 (1.9%)	0	1	0	1 (4%)
Other	0	1 (1.9%)	0	0	0	0
Totals	18 (100%)	53 (100%)	10	7	8	25 (100%)

Table 6. The Expert Commission: Members and Structure

Choosing actors	Institution	Chosen members (XX = regular participation; X = irregular participation or limited membership; I = interviewed)	Position at time of commission's work	Educational background	Former professional positions/functions
	State Department of Justice, Northern Westphalia	R (XX, I)	Director of the Section for Economic Crime; Initiator of Specialized Prosecutor's System	Lawyer	
	State Department of Justice, Bavaria	O (XX, I)	Director of the Criminal Law Department	Lawyer	Prosecutor; criminal court judge
	Police	K (XX, I)	Director of the Economic Crime Department	Police education, uncompleted law studies	Police career; since 1948 Economic Crime Department
		Tr (X)	FBI, Director for economic crime	Police education	Police career
		replaced by N (X, I)	FBI	Lawyer; police education	
	State attorneys	D (X, I)	General state attorney (retired)	Lawyer	Prosecutor; criminal court
Federal Department of Justice, Section for Criminal Justice		W (XX, I)	Chief state attorney	Lawyer	Prosecutor; criminal court judge; chair of the Commission for the Criminal Code Reform
		E (X)	State attorney	Lawyer	15 Years prosecutor for economic offenses

Group	Code	Position	Profession/Training	Career background
Federal Supreme Court	Kl (XX)	State attorney for economic crime	Lawyer	
	P (XX, I)	Appeal Judge with the Supreme Court; Chair of the First Appellate Criminal Court	Lawyer	Judge; assistant with the Supreme Court, Civil Law Section of the Bavarian Department of Justice
Association of Certified Public Accountants	Sch (XX, I)	Certified public accountant	Business administration	
West German Lawyers Assn.	SL	Defense attorney	Lawyer	Reichsjustizministerium
Academics	T (XX, I)	Professor and Director of Institute (criminal law and criminology)	Lawyer	Academic career
	U (XX, I)	Professor and Director of Institute (economic law)	Lawyer	Academic career
	B (X, I)	Professor and Director of Institute (economic/ trade law)	Lawyer	Academic career
	Ra (XX, I)	Professor (economic/ trust law)	Lawyer	Federal Department of Justice, Section for Criminal Justice; Academic career
Politicians, factions of the Bundestag	One representative each faction of the Bundestag, no appearance except:		Lawyers	
	DN (XX)	Defense attorney; former FDP-Rep.	Lawyer	

ocratic (SPD)-governed North Rhine-Westphalia, and member B from Christian Social Union (CSU)-governed Bavaria. Two police persons became members. One of them, member K, was the head of the police department for economic crime of a major city. The other, member Tr, was responsible for economic crime in the Federal Bureau of Investigation (*Bundeskriminalamt*, BKA). Due to organizational shifts in the BKA, Tr was later replaced by another colleague, member N. Four prosecutors were among the commissioners. One of them, former state attorney general D, originally chaired the commission. After his withdrawal from the commission W, then chief prosecutor of a major city, took over the chair. Member P, president of a criminal court chamber of the Federal Supreme Court,[4] was the only judge in the commission. Sch, a certified public accountant, was the only economist. He had been suggested to the Justice Department by his professional organization. Member SL, the only defense attorney in the commission, attended only one of the meetings. Four scholars were among the members. T was a professor of criminal law, specializing in economic crime. Members U, B, and Ra participated as professors of economic and trade law (T, U, and B were also directors of highly reputed research institutes). In addition, each of the factions of the *Bundestag* (Christian Democratic Union/Christian Social Union [CDU/CSU], Free Democratic Party [FPD], Social Democratic Party [SPD]) were invited to nominate a member of parliament and one substitute for the commission. The representatives, however, never attended the meetings, except for former Representative DN who had been nominated by the libertarian FPD faction. Except for this one actor, the parliament was not engaged in any of the commission's decisions until the end of this phase.

With few exceptions, members of the commission were lawyers by education; only the one economist and two policemen were not. One of the latter had not completed any advanced academic education.

Characteristics of the commission's membership do not sufficiently tell us about the types of knowledge that became relevant in the course of the negotiations. We need to learn about the relative chances of communication and the influence of the representatives from different social spheres. Those who define the culture and the language of the commission have better access to communication processes. Their success shows that they were more influential, and it can be assumed that their influence further increased after these successful definition processes.

In order to learn about the position of different actors in the com-

---

4. The *Bundesgerichtshof* is the Federal Supreme Court for civil and criminal law cases.

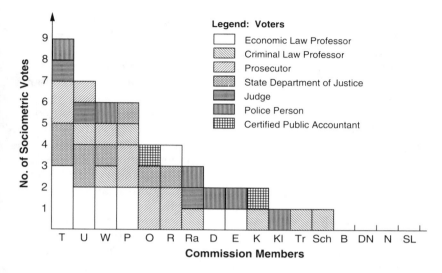

Figure 3. Sociometric positions and votes within the expert commission.

munication structure, we investigated the sociometric status of the participants. We asked each interviewed member with which other members he (only "he" interviewees included) had had the most intensive and frequent communication in the course of the commission's work. Figure 3 shows the distribution of "votes" which the twelve interviewed members gave to other members of the commission.

Commissioners most often named T, the criminal law professor, as one of their most frequent communication partners (9 times). This indicates his influential position, supported by the decisions on the commission's program. More than two-thirds of the issues chosen had been listed by T at the meetings of the Lawyers Association. This influence may be due to T's precise knowledge of and adaptation to the needs of the criminal justice system, particularly the prosecutors. Yet, with this reservation, his case shows that one highly motivated and knowledgeable actor can be extraordinarily influential up to this stage of a law preparation process. The second highest number of "votes" (7) were given to member U, the professor for economic law. He was followed by state attorney W (6), who chaired the commission for most of its duration and took an important coordinative and integrative position. An equal number of votes were given to supreme court justice P. Four votes were given to O and R, the members of the State Departments of Justice. Both had an important function formulating numerous provisions discussed by the commission and later suggested to the law makers. They were followed by the professor for economic law Ra (3); by two prosecutors and one policeman, D, E, and K (2 each); and by the prosecutor Kl, the policeman Tr, and the certified public accountant Sch (1 each). No votes were given to the one former parliamentarian, to the third policeman, to the third professor for economic law, and to the defense attorney.

The sociometric status of the different members may be caused by several factors: intensity of personal involvement, expertise, frequency of participation and length of membership, sharing of the dominant culture and language, and gender. The latter of these variables could help to explain the isolation of the only female member of the commission, Rep. DN, who attended every meeting and is an experienced lawyer and politician. The other three with no votes either did not attend the meetings very frequently or were not members for the entire duration of the commission. The same is true for three of the six who got only one or two votes, but for only one of the seven who received three or more votes.

Sharing of the dominant legal culture and language is another important factor explaining the sociometric status of different commissioners. Non-lawyers received few votes or none at all. This relevance of common language and shared knowledge can be illustrated by a quotation from the transcribed interviews. A policeman said:

> Well, I was a lawyer, for three years with an attorney. . . . But here [with the police, J. J. S.] you forget all that. You practically become just a policeperson. . . . I must say, I had some problems there [in the commission, J. J. S.]. . . . Also the way they worked there was really new for me. . . . There was the other colleague from the police. He really didn't understand anything. He sat there and never said a word. Well, he was no lawyer. He sometimes only shook his head.

Other factors than the lack of or distance from university education may also isolate a member. The one economist and certified public accountant in the commission stressed that "the other members of the commission had no relation to money," and thus misjudged, for example, conditions for the fraudulant creation of firms with limited liability. The commission's suggestion to raise the legal minimum for the foundation of such firms from 20,000 to 50,000 German marks appeared "ridiculous" to him. He pleaded, unsuccessfully, for a minimum capital of 200,000 German marks.

Figure 3 also makes distinctions among the "voters." The numerous votes given by T, the "sociometric star," are remarkable. T named people at the fringe as well as the center of the sociometric hierarchy. As a criminal law professor and specialist for economic crime, he had

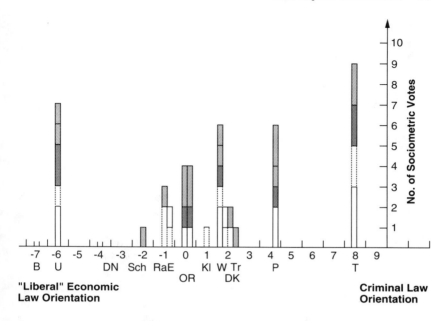

Figure 4. Positions of members of the expert commission on the pro-/anti-criminalization scale.

tried (particularly in the beginning), to form a coalition of criminal law-related members. His strategy was to gain them as supporters of his proposals, against the opposition of the economic law proponents. In later stages T's relations shifted toward his academic colleagues. Still, the conflict line between the criminal law proponents and the economic lawyers remained. N, who entered the commission only late, stated: "T was very active there. And so was U. The two always had heavy disputes." In answer to our question about the main conflict line in the commission, almost all members pointed to that between pro-criminalizers and anti-criminalizers. Antitrust law, bookkeeping regulations, submission law, and bankruptcy law were named as the most critical issues. Figure 4 shows how often different members were referred to on each question, and who was on which side. If members got positive (pro-criminalization) and negative (anti-criminalization) votes, these were subtracted from each other.

Commissioners T and U, the criminal law and economic law professors, both of whom got the most sociometric votes, were referred to as the heaviest fighters for criminal law and economic law rationales respectively. Only one of the other economic law professors was more extreme on the liberal side. The libertarian party politician DN was also far to this side of the scale. Other members on the economic law side were the third economic lawyer, the economist, and one state attorney. On the criminal law side, the judge and all other state attorneys and police persons joined T. The two members of the State Departments of Justice were considered to be in a neutral position.

Cognitive Maps of Experts

The representation of certain position holders in the consultation process does not guarantee that their knowledge and rationality become relevant in an expert commission, as we have seen. Equally so, the nonparticipation of other position holders does not necessarily mean the exclusion of their rationalities. Economic lawyers, for example, represent profound economic knowledge. Criminal law professors may be well qualified to represent the perspective of empirical criminology or criminal sociology. It is an empirical question whether they actually do so. To answer this question for our case, we analyzed the cognitions implied in different contributions of participants in the commission and in the hearing.

We applied the cognitive mapping approach, as described above (see Chapter 2), to documents from the commission's meetings and to minutes from the parliamentary hearing. We thus identified argument structures of the participants. In addition, we developed indicators from these maps that allow for a comparison of a diversity of maps from different sources, different actors, and different points in time.

Before discussing and comparing indicators of various terms of rationality for a greater number of actors, we now analyze two individual cognitive maps. They represent the highly complex argumentation structures of the most significant representatives and sociometric stars of the two "camps" within the commission: commissioner U for the economic-law side, and commissioner T for the criminal-law side. The topic is one of the most crucial issues of the commission's work: the criminalization of severe cases of price-fixing and trust-related behavior. Economic law professor U's discussion of this topic, 44 pages in length, reacts to the 227-page expert opinion of criminal law professor T. U's text is a differentiated analysis of the causes and consequences of trust-related behavior, and of positively and negatively evaluated consequences of different types of administrative and criminal law regulations. His cognitive map contains 34 different concepts and 30 different causal assumptions. Five different graphs (distinct sets of causal relations) can be distinguished, the three more complex of which are represented in Figure 5. They could be called "problem graph," "free

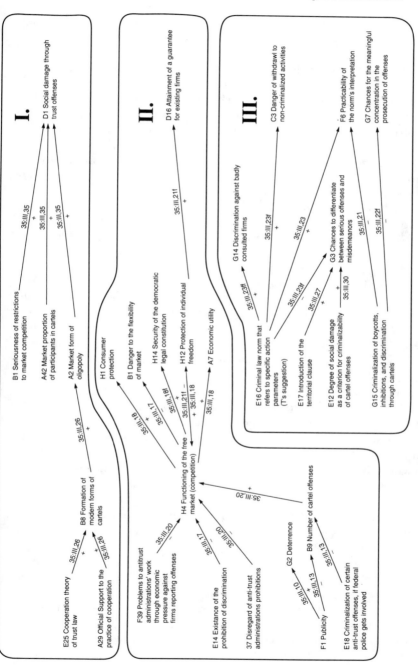

Figure 5. Cognitive map of economic law professor U on the criminalization of trust-related offenses.

market graph," and "criminal justice graph." While we cannot engage in a detailed discussion of these graphs, we wish to summarize briefly the basic logic of each of them.

The "problem graph" (I in Figure 5) outlines U's understanding of the emergence and consequences of trusts. U first outlines the conditions of modern types of trusts, including government support for the cooperation between competitors. Such trusts further increase the probability of oligopolic markets in which (in a final step) trust offenses with highly problematic social consequences are likely to occur. This graph thus contains mainly economic arguments and points to the presently high probability of antitrust offenses and their negative consequences.

The "free market graph" (II in Figure 5), which is the most complex graph in this cognitive map, is named for its core concept, the functioning of free competition. U discusses control conditions under which free competition is likely to function and the consequences of free markets. Several technical conditions of administrative control are considered deficient and contribute, U argues, to challenges of the free market, for example through price-fixing behavior. The publicity often achieved by the antitrust administration is considered an effective weapon against antitrust offenses. While it increases deterrence, the same publicity effect may be achieved through agencies of criminal justice. In general, the criminalization of severe offenses under specified conditions is expected to contribute to a decrease of offense behavior, and thereby to increase the functioning of the free market. With regard to the consequences of market competition, U argues that a functioning market is a central condition for a variety of social goods: protection of consumers, stabilization of the democratic and legal state constitution, protection of individual liberty (too much of which, however, could endanger the functioning of the market), and finally economic prosperity in general. Whereas the key position in this graph of an economic concept, the free market system, is not surprising for an economic law scholar, his implicit plea for a qualified criminalization of trust offenses does not fit with the idea of U as the main anti-criminalizer of the commission.

The third complex set of arguments, the "criminal justice graph," helps to solve this paradox (III in Figure 5). Here U analyzes in a more differentiated way several positive and negative impacts of alternatively worded provisions. For example, the reference to specific action parameters (prices, quantities, and scope of markets) in the definition of the criminal offense may allow firms to withdraw to forms of behavior that are not covered by the criminal law provision, but that may nevertheless be harmful to markets. Such a provision would also make it difficult to differentiate between serious offenses and misdemeanors. On the other hand, specificity increases the practicability and applicability of the provision. Introducing the degree of social harm as a criterion for the criminalizability of cartel offenses improves the chances of differentiating between serious offenses and misdemeanors. The same holds for the territorial condition, which requires that an offense must affect the entire jurisdiction of the federal law in order to constitute a criminal offense. On the other hand, the criminalization of boycotts, inhibitions, and discrimination (by market participants against other market participants) decreases the practicability of the criminal provision and would also wear on a meaningfully focused prosecution of serious offenses. In sum, whereas the two central specifications of criminalization are evaluated positively, a third specification is expected to have negative consequences for the effective use of criminal law, and a fourth is evaluated ambivalently. The specifications in U's position and the limitations of criminalizing provisions for which he fought, may have created his reputation as an anti-criminalizer with the other members of the commission. In general, U argues as an economist and lawyer. The key variable of his analysis or the dominant criterion of rationality, however, is clearly economic: the functioning of the free market as a central condition for the economic and political fate of society.

The document of the criminal law scholar T is a 227-page expert opinion on the same topic. T proposes 168 concepts and 141 causal relations. A cognitive map of this complexity can no longer be graphically reconstructed in its full size. In order to enable a limited comparison, however, we have reduced and drawn T's cognitive map for the more interesting graphs and for those variables that he shares with U and two other experts who contributed to this topic; included are all concepts connected by one causal step with the shared variables.

T's cognitive map shows six different graphs. A very complex graph is surrounded by five limited ones. Two of these rather short graphs can be seen on the lower left of Figure 6. One of them shows several conditions that result in social harm from potential antitrust offenses, including the nonfunctioning of the price system as a measure of scarcity, the delusion of competitive market conditions, the durability of certain types of cartels, and the loss of free market principles (I in Figure 6). The next graph shows that any necessity to prove the occurrence of social damage from antitrust offenses as a condition for punishability results in negative consequences, including uncertainties in the legal process (II in Figure 6). On the upper left, one graph points to the ineffectiveness of the present administrative antitrust system, mainly resulting from the chances of offenders to shift fines over to

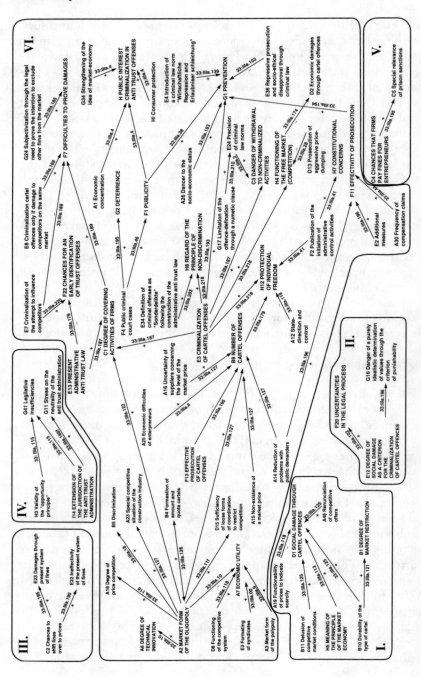

Figure 6. Cognitive map of criminal law professor `T on the criminalization of trust-related offenses.

consumers through price increases (III in Figure 6). According to another graph (IV in Figure 6), the extension of administrative control authority would not be an adequate solution. It would, instead, strain the neutrality of the antitrust administration. The last simple graph (V on the lower right of Figure 6) documents T's belief in the creation of a prison sanction for trust offenders, since other types of sanctions (e.g., fines) could be compensated by the firms.

These short graphs indicate several important facts. Criminal law professor T shows an intimate knowledge of economic behavior and of the functioning of the present control system. He is far from limiting his line of arguments to legal dogmatic issues. His text clearly stresses the negative aspects of the administrative control system. And, in the last graph, T documents his belief in the effectiveness of criminal sanctions, including imprisonment. T thus confirms the other commissioners' characterization of his role as the main proponent of criminalization.

The very complex graph (VI covering most of the map in Figure 6) shows five key concepts within the complex lines of argumentation. The left side of the graph is dominated by economic analysis. Here the key concepts are the oligopolic market, economic utility, and the number of trust-related offenses. The evaluation of oligopolies is ambivalent, involving positive and negative impacts. Although oligopolies are regarded as possible promoters of technical development and of price competition, they are also thought to cause economic harm and increase the likelihood of antitrust offenses (the second and third key concepts of the economic part of this graph). The concept of offenses most clearly connects the economic part of the graph with the criminal justice part. Key concepts are the criminalization and prevention of offenses. Criminalization is mostly discussed in terms of its positive consequences, such as the protection of individual liberty, the functioning of the free market system, the prevention of antitrust offenses, and the guarantee of legal equality. Negative consequences are only seen in entrepreneurial attempts to prevent criminalization through tactical measures. These, however, could be partly prevented through a specification of the criminal provision. T sees many more immediate positive consequences of criminalization of trust offenses than the economic lawyer U. In U's case the majority of advantages were explained through the intervening variable "functioning of the free market." T's central graph demonstrates two more major lines of reasoning that lead to "prevention." In one of them the preventive impact of the publicity of public criminal law suits is stressed. The other points to several conditions that would increase the efficacy of prosecution.

The discussion of the cognitive map of criminal jurisprudent T shows, despite the use of numerous economic arguments, a much clearer criminal justice orientation than the map of the economic lawyer. T makes a much stronger point in favor of criminalization. Most noteworthy, criminal justice and justice (e.g., equality in law) principles predominate as target concepts. Despite considerable references to economic thinking, legal rationales dominate T's reasoning.

The cognitive maps of T and U were described and interpreted in terms of their basic structures and concepts. Not all their arguments can be interpreted here. Instead the detailed analysis of individual maps should be supplemented by a comparative perspective. We can compare a multitude of cognitive maps only if we reduce their complexity. For this reason we have developed indicators that express the quality of several dimensions of maps in a numerical value. The dimensions in which we are interested are related to the two types of rationality distinguished above.

Purposive rationality (*Zweckrationalität*), according to Weber, is that aspect of the action orientation that considers the intended and unintended consequences of different action or policy alternatives, impacts on the policy purposes, and possible side effects. Only after considering their costs and benefits will the rational actor decide for one or the other action or policy alternative. Several indicators that clarify the purposive rationality of experts are listed in Table 7.

When actors consider the impacts of policy alternatives in a complex societal field, they must consider a large number of variables. The consideration of a high number of variables is therefore a necessary condition for purposive rational acting. Column 3 of Table 7 shows the number of concepts or variables used by different actors (a) of the expert commission on the criminalization of several trust-related offenses and (b) at the later parliamentary hearing on price fixing when the issue had already been narrowed down to bid-rigging cases. The next column, 4, standardizes the number of concepts per situation by setting the maximum value of each situation equal to one hundred. In the following column, 5, all concepts are related to the maximum number of concepts used in one single cognitive map for all situations (168 = 100%). It turns out that the value differs greatly within each situation. The average value, however, is much higher for the expert commission (42) than for the hearing (8.34), which could be explained by the more extended time and space available in the commission. In these terms the commission is the better place for a thorough assessment of policy impacts.

If we compare the situation-specific values for the hearing, we find that the academics do not have the highest value. The highest values are for the representatives of industry and the trust control administra-

TABLE 7. Purposive Rationality of Experts

1. Situation	2. Actors (code no.)	3. co (no. of concepts)	4. Co-indicator/situation-specific = $\frac{co \times 100}{\text{max. no. co in situation}}$	5. Co-indicator (general) = $\frac{co \times 100}{\text{max. no. co}}$	6. pa = no. of pages of text	7. $\frac{co}{pa}$	8. rel: no. of causal relations	9. Index of causal integration (ioci) = $\frac{rel}{co}$
Expert commission	T (33)	168	100	100	227	0.74	141	0.84
	G (34)	64	38	38	51	1.25	61	0.97
	U (35)	34	20	20	44	0.78	30	0.90
	St (36)	14	9	9	16	0.88	10	0.71
	averages	70	42	42	85	0.91	61	0.85
Hearing								
Professors	M (10)	9	35	5.4	5	1.8	6	0.66
	F (9)	20	78	12	6.5	3.0	16	0.8
	averages	14.5	56.5	8.7	5.75	2.5	11	0.78
Industry	Fr (7)	26	100	15.6	8.5	3.1	30	1.2
	B (6)	13	50	7.8	2.8	4.6	10	0.8
	averages	19.5	75	11.7	5.65	3.2	20	1.0
Criminal justice	Be (11)	13	50	7.8	4.5	2.9	13	1.0
	L (5)	6	23.5	3.6	6	1.0	3	0.5
	N (4)	13	50	7.8	8	1.6	13	1.0
	averages	10.7	41.2	6.4	6.2	1.3	10	0.9
Trust control administration	A (3)	16	62	9.6	7.5	2.1	10	0.6
	K (2)	23	92	13.8	11.2	2.1	19	0.8
	averages	19.5	77	11.7	9.35	2.1	15	0.7
Averages		15.3	60	8.34	5.9	2.5	13.3	0.82

tion. These actors are the most interested in the prevention of the proposition under consideration. Among these actors, Fr, the representative of the construction industry, which is the main target group of the proposed norm, has the highest value. A correlation exists between interests involved and variables included. This points once more to the fact that using "number of concepts" as the indicator for purposive rationality can only be understood as expressing a necessary condition for purposive rationality. It does not inform us about the numbers of social spheres from which variables have been considered. It also does not express how well different types of impacts of a policy have been considered.

Column 6 of Table 7 lists the number of pages of each document. Column 7 relates the number of concepts to the number of pages of the documents analyzed. A comparison between the two situations proves that the more limited are time and space, the more concentrated is the argumentation. This indicator also shows the highest values for the most interested groups: industry, which fears a criminalization of entrepreneurs; and the trust control administration, which fears a loss of control in favor of the criminal justice system. The number of causal relations per cognitive map is shown in column 8. In column 9 the number of causal relations is related to the number of concepts used. It expresses how thoroughly possible causal relations between the concepts used are discussed by each actor. These values can be understood as indexes of the causal integration within each cognitive map. We do not find any correlation between these indexes and the number of concepts, although the number of logically possible causal relations increases as an exponential function of the number of concepts. The only obvious result of this column is, again, the highest value for the most interested actor, the representative of the construction industry.

The fact that the most interested actors have the highest "argumentative strength" directs our attention to the *substantive rationalities* that underlie their argumentations. We have distinguished different types of arguments and counted their absolute and relative weight within the argumentation of each individual actor (see Table 8). Earlier, units under investigation were concepts or variables; now they are causal relations. They are distinguished according to four categories: arguments that (1) explain offenses, (2) express negatively evaluated impacts of criminalization, (3) point to negatively evaluated impacts of offenses, and (4) indicate positive impacts of criminalization. Whereas the former two arguments tend to imply an anti-criminalization tendency, the latter two tend to imply a pro-criminalization tendency. Within each of the four types of arguments, we further distinguished economic, legal, and other ones. The arguments that do not fit into these categories are counted as "other arguments."

When we first look at the distribution of arguments for the cognitive maps of T and U analyzed above, we find that both use more "pro-criminalization" than "anti-criminalization" arguments. For T these are 41 percent as opposed to 17 percent; 41 percent of T's arguments did not fit in one of the categories. For U we find 57 percent "pro-criminalization" arguments as opposed to 23 percent "anti-criminalization" arguments. Here only 20 percent of the causal relations did not fit any category. Most of T's arguments point to negative economic impacts of offenses (17%), and to positive legal consequences of criminalization (16%). These types of arguments are followed by causal relations that point to economic explanations of offenses (11%). This latter type stands for most of T's "anti-criminalization" factors, the "weakest" type within this general category. U mostly points to the negative economic impacts of trust offenses (37%), then to positive legal impacts of criminalization (13%). These "pro-criminalization" arguments are opposed by others when U discusses negative economic (10%) and legal (7%) impacts of criminalization.

The maps of the parliamentary hearing show a different pattern. Economic law professor M, taking an anti-criminalization perspective, concentrates almost all his arguments on the economic explanation of offenses (83%). Economics professor F mostly explains their negative economic impacts (50%) and supports criminalization. Professor M had been suggested by the (anti-criminalization) CDU/CSU faction, Professor F by the (pro-criminalization) SPD faction. The scholars participating at the hearings take more polarized positions than their counterparts at the expert commission.

Representatives of interest groups take even more one-sided perspectives: 100 percent of the arguments of both speakers for industry associations are "anti-criminalization" arguments. Both almost exclusively try to explain offenses with economic reasoning. The remaining causal relations refer to negative impacts of criminalization. Speakers of the trust control administration also concentrate most of their arguments on the anti-criminalization side. They thus support their administration's official position and organization maintenance interests. One of them explains the offenses (70%), while the other one stresses negative legal impacts of criminalization (63%). Two of the representatives of the criminal justice sector support the pro-criminalization perspective (85% and 69%), and the third distributes his arguments in equal parts. They, too, support the policy alternative that appears rational within their frame of reference, that is, within the general

TABLE 8. Substantive Rationalities of Experts by Types of Arguments (N/proportion)

Situation / Type of argument / Actor	All arguments	(Pro-criminalization implications)									(Anti-criminalization implications)									Other arguments
		Negative impacts of offenses				Negative impacts of criminalization				Totals	Explanatory arguments for offenses				Positive impacts of criminalization				Totals	
		Economic	Legal	Other	Totals	Economic	Legal	Other	Totals		Economic	Legal	Other	Totals	Economic	Legal	Other	Totals		
Expert commission																				
T (33)	141	16/0.11			16/0.11		6/0.04	2/0.01	8/0.06	24/0.17	24/0.17	4/0.03	1/0.01	29/0.20	4/0.03	22/0.16	3/0.02	29/0.20	58/0.41	59/0.41
G (34)	61						4/0.07		4/0.07	4/0.07	3/0.05	2/0.03		5/0.08		3/0.05		3/0.05	8/0.13	49/0.80
U (35)	30		2/0.07		2/0.07	2/0.07	3/0.10		5/0.17	7/0.23	11/0.37	2/0.07		13/0.43		4/0.13		4/0.13	17/0.57	6/0.20
St (36)	10																			10/1
Totals	242	16/0.07	2/0.01		18/0.07	2/0.01	13/0.05	2/0.01	17/0.07	35/0.14	38/0.16	8/0.03	1/0.004	47/0.19	4/0.02	29/0.12	3/0.01	36/0.15	83/0.34	124/0.51
Hearing																				
M (10) law	6	5/0.83			5/0.83					5/0.83										1/0.17
F (9) economics	16	3/0.19			3/0.19					3/0.19	8/0.5			8/0.5					8/0.5	5/0.31

	N												
Totals: academia	22	8/0.36							8/0.36	8/0.36	8/0.36	8/0.36	6/0.28
Fr (7) construction industry	30	27/0.9	1/0.01	2/0.05	1/0.03	3/0.1	8/0.36	30/1					
B (6) industry federation	10	8/0.8		1/0.1	1/0.1	2/0.2		10/1					
Totals: industry	40	35/0.88	1/0.03	3/0.08	1/0.03	5/0.13		40/1					
Be (11) FBI	13	2/0.15					1/0.08	2/0.15	1/0.08		1/0.08	11/0.85	1/0.33
L (5)	3			1/0.33	1/0.33	1/0.33		1/0.33		1/0.33	1/0.33	1/0.33	
N (4)	13			1/0.07	1/0.07	2/0.15	1/0.07	2/0.15	5/0.38	1/0.07	8/0.61	9/0.69	2/0.15
Totals: prosecutors	16			1/0.06	2/0.13	3/0.19	1/0.07	2/0.15	6/0.38	1/0.06	9/0.56	10/0.63	3/0.19
A (3)	10	2/0.2	3/0.3	2/0.2			7/0.7	7/0.7					3/0.7
K (2)	19	4/0.21		12/0.61	1/0.03	13/0.45	17/0.89						2/0.11
Totals: trust-control-adm.	29	6/0.2	3/0.1	2/0.2	11/0.38	12/0.42	1/0.03	13/0.45	24/0.82	13/0.45			5/0.17

purpose orientation of their organizational settings, and that would expand the field of control of their organization.

Industry, Experts, and Antitrust Law by Peter Brühl

The commission first debated antitrust offenses at its eighth session (November 25–29, 1974). The commissioners heard testimony from several experts, attempting to discover if additional administrative or criminal penalties were needed to secure consumer protection and functioning markets. "Criminalization of antitrust offenses" was then scheduled for the tenth session in October 1975.

Industry associations first became involved during the preparation of the eighth meeting. The initial contact resulted from the personal relation between Professor Tiedemann and Dr. M of the German Federation of Industry (BDI), and was established as early as the 49th meetings of the Lawyers Association. Tiedemann prepared his trust control proposal for the commission during Winter Semester 1973/74 at the Criminological Institute of Freiburg University. He invited "one representative each of the BDI, the German Union Federation (*Deutscher Gewerkschafts-Bund, DGB*), and the Federal Trust Control Agency (*Bundeskartellamt*)" (BDI, archival document). In his lecture of January 15, 1974, Dr. M discussed the redefinition of administrative anti-trust regulations into criminal laws. He strongly opposed such a move and found the reactions of seminar participants to be critical of his views, "as was to be expected" (BDI, archival document).

Two days after his lecture, on January 17, 1974, Dr. M informed the members of the BDI working group on antitrust law that the expert commission would, "toward the end of its deliberations, under the category of especially difficult issues, also consider the redefinition of some antitrust offenses into criminal offenses. . . . Even though the majority of commissioners did not favor deliberations on this issue, Professors T and U had successfully insisted" (BDI, archival document). Dr. M enclosed a copy of the lecture he had given at Professor T's seminar and a summary of the participants' critical arguments.

The second attempt to influence the commission's work derived from a personal relationship between Dr. M (BDI) and Judge K, president of the Berlin Court of Appeals. Judge K had been invited to give testimony at the eighth session of the expert commission. In a letter to Dr. M, he enclosed a copy of the session's itinerary. He stated that he was only superficially informed about the issues at stake and would only be able to talk about his court experience with administrative fees against antitrust offenses. On October 25, 1974 Dr. M sent Judge K a copy of the lecture he had given at Professor T's seminar. His cover letter stated that, according to his impressions at Freiburg, Professor T would not favor criminalizing antitrust offenses. Despite this correspondence, Judge K argued at the eighth session that criminalizing some antitrust offenses would be logically unavoidable given the current criminalization of misleading advertising (Bundesministerium der Justiz 1975, Appendix 8, 1).

The BDI also had an opportunity to address the commission directly since the director of its department for legal affairs was invited to speak at the eighth session. After consulting with Dr. M, however, this director did not speak to issues of antitrust law (Bundesministerium der Justiz 1974, Appendix 1, 7). Commissioners nevertheless asked about the paper Dr. M had given at Professor T's seminar and requested that the BDI send an official statement on antitrust issues. Such a statement was subsequently submitted by Dr. M. It became part of the commission's record as the "statement of the German Federation of Industry, delivered after the eighth session for the preparation of future deliberations" (Bundesministerium der Justiz 1975, X).

In November 1974 the commission had scheduled the issue of antitrust offenses for its tenth session, to be held in October 1975. Prior to this session, Dr. M of the BDI was again invited to speak to a seminar Professor T was teaching on "Antitrust Offenses and Criminal Law." Dr. M was asked to comment on some legislative proposals drafted by a private group of law professors in March 1975. These proposals included one to criminalize antitrust offenses. In a letter to the members of the working group on antitrust issues, Dr. M reported these new developments and the proposals of the academic group. He stated again that the use of pressure and fraudulent misrepresentation was already covered by present criminal law, rendering criminalization in the area of antitrust law superfluous. Yet "we are confronted with the tactical choice to agree to such a proposal in order to prevent further reaching requests for criminalizations in the antitrust area. We request comments from those member associations who commonly bid for the production of goods and services" (letter by Dr. M).

The BDI files contained only a single response from April 22, 1975, given by the chair of the antitrust work group of the Association of Automobile Producers. This statement strongly urged dropping discussion of antitrust offenses, arguing that [there is] hardly anything psychologically and politically worse," since this debate [is] highly charged with emotions." On April 30, 1975 Dr. M sent the draft of his lecture for Professor T's seminar to members of the BDI working group on antitrust law, requesting critical comments. In this paper he strongly rejected all proposals the professorial work group had developed on the criminalization of antitrust offenses. Four responses Dr. M received on his draft are documented in BDI files, including one by the Association of Chemical Industries and one by Esso Corporation. All statements support Dr. M's defensive strategy.

In a meeting of the BDI working group on antitrust law on May 13, 1975, Dr. M presented an "overview of the motives for the attempted criminalization of antitrust offenses, to be sought in motivations of social ethics." In the subsequent debate, group members expressed their concerns that, "given presently dominant trends in society," such criminalization might be hard to prevent. They concluded though that "the suitable time for cooperation on compromise formulas has not yet come."

The night of this same day, Dr. M lectured to the seminar of Professor and Commissioner T in Freiburg, expressing his opposition to the professor's proposal. According to BDI files, this was his only attempt to influence the commission's proceedings after the paper he had submitted in late 1974. The only other information about contacts between industry and the commission is contained in a letter Dr. M wrote to Dr. W of the Daimler-Benz corporation. Here Dr. M refers to an earlier letter from this Daimler-Benz executive (April 7, 1975), in which Dr. W had offered to talk with Professor and Commissioner U at a meeting before the tenth conference of the commission. M offered his assistance, commenting that U had, "in recent times, demonstrated more of his progressive side." At a panel discussion in Berlin on intercorporate cooperation, he had been tougher than the two participating speakers of the federal antitrust agency, according to Dr. M's letter. "We agree that this does not diminish the necessity to cultivate an ongoing relation."

At its tenth conference the expert commission for the fight against economic crime passed several suggestions to criminalize antitrust offenses previously regulated by administrative law. The suggestions included criminalizing bid rigging in cases where fraudulent behavior had been initiated but not yet occurred (Bundesministerium der Justiz 1976). The commission largely followed the wording suggested by the professorial work group, according to which the action of potential bidders providing or promising advantages to other competitors, or who deluded, or threatened them, were covered by the proposition and would be punished with up to three years of imprisonment.

The commission's decisions openly challenged the interests of the business sector. It is uncertain to what degree the lack of testimony at the commission's tenth session was due to the industry's strategy not to engage in the debate or due to the will of commissioners to keep lobbying groups out of the deliberations. In response to our question,

Dr. M from the BDI did regret that no members of the business associations or corporations had been nominated as commissioners.

In sum, the industrial sector was not directly represented in the commission. Communications between the commission and business were rare and mostly indirect. Dr. M's statement to the commission was the only direct communication. Indirect communications were not successful. They changed neither votes of those commissioners at whom they had been directed (T and U) nor testimonies (W) in the desired direction. The final vote of the commission on the criminalization of bid rigging was unanimous. The business sector, in short, had been unsuccessful in influencing a rather autonomous expert commission.

Preliminary Conclusions on Experts: Primacy and Autonomy of Criminal Justice

The quality of experts that are admitted to the law-making process tends to reflect the interests and perspectives of the institution initiating the process. Lawyers in the Criminal Justice Division of the Federal Department of Justice had composed a commission dominated by lawyers and representatives of the criminal justice sector. The dominant agenda for the solution of economic deviance was thereby established through an early selection process which reflected public sentiments and the opportunity of political gain. This agenda was focused on law and criminal justice. Those members of the commission who were not lawyers experienced considerable communication problems in the commission. We could not determine whether this was due to their lack of academic or, more specifically, legal education. Lawyers who had expertise in relevant nonlegal fields—economics and criminology—brought this knowledge into the debate.[5] On the other hand, social scientists such as sociologists, economists, and criminologists were left out.

The legislature only became involved quite late in the law-making process and in the choice of experts. When they did, the weight of experts from lobbying groups grew within the total group of experts. The arguments of experts were, at this point, more clearly oriented toward the realization of their organizations' or professions' interests than in earlier stages.

5. This points to the potential relevance of the inclusion of economic and sociological knowledge in legal education. Particularly given the increasing intrusion of nonlegal substantive rationales in legal issues characterizing our case and others, the rational consideration of economic and sociological reasoning is a necessary condition for the achievement of purposive rationality in policy formation.

In sum, the process of expert consultation during the commission's tenure was relatively autonomous, unhampered by lobbying groups. This does not mean, however, that it was free of bias. The frame of reference had been determined at the outset to be criminal justice. This emphasis on criminal justice strategies was backed by public sentiment.

Chapter 5
The Production of the Second Law Against Economic Crime: The Political Sector

Binding decisions on the criminalization of economic deviance are not made by experts but in the political process. While the political sector made use of the commission's recommendations, it also transformed and restructured them. A draft bill, first developed by the Justice Department, progressed into the legislature, was modified several times under the pressure of industrial lobbying groups, and finally was enacted. This chapter describes the political process. We first relate this process, in a brief introduction, to our theoretical model.

Functionality and Social Action in the Political Sector

Holistic and functionalist assumptions concerning the political sector are as problematic as those concerning the economy or capital. Social action within the political system needs to be taken into consideration when we want to explain the criminalization of behavior by political decision makers. To clarify this point it is helpful to look briefly at a most insightful analysis of the Austrian criminal code reform of the 1960s (Stangl 1985). Stangl criticizes von Hippel's (1898) classical argument that the emergence of prisons in the nineteenth century resulted from increasingly negative attitudes toward the cruelty of previous systems of corporal punishment and from an initial insight into the uselessness of previous methods of criminal justice. Stangl rightfully stresses that this argument leaves two major questions unexplained: first, why such a "rejection" and "insight" grew in the historical situation analyzed; and second, why they became relevant in political decision making. An adequate understanding of the development of criminal law is only possible, Stangl argues, if processes in the political system itself are analyzed.

> Political processes withdraw from a simple logic of functional needs and social action. They reformulate objective problems and societal needs and interests into problems of power. As a consequence, political action typically has impacts that may be contradictory to the needs of the socio-cultural and/or economic system. (Stangl 1985, p. 19)

By this line of argument, it is not the problems themselves that initiate political reform but the power interests that connect political parties with underlying claims making. Stangl argues that

> in analogy to the capitalist logic of production . . . , that from the perspective of parties . . . it is not the use value (*Gebrauchswert*) of reforms that counts, but the political exchange value, i.e., the realization of party power against the political opponent. (Stangl 1985, p. 21)

Stangl's demand that processes within the political system must be investigated in order to understand the genesis of criminal law corresponds to our approach. Criminal law just does not automatically adapt to presumed needs of society or the economic system. Yet, while Stangl criticizes functionalist "explanations," in the tradition of Rusche and Kirchheimer, a close analysis of his approach shows that he introduces a new type of functionalist reasoning himself. Whereas publications of "left functionalism" aim at the explanation of criminal law making through the functions it fulfills for the process of capital accumulation, Stangl wants to explain it through the functions it fulfills for the process of political party power accumulation. Stangl simply exchanges functional criteria external to the political system by ones that are internal.

If it is correct that the second criterion (power accumulation) is more important in the rationales of political decision makers than the first (capital accumulation) or other functional criteria (e.g., justice), then indeed it will impact more strongly on the outcome of criminal legislation. The relative importance of these functional criteria, however, is an empirical question. In more general terms, which social forces determine which political actors in what situations on what issues prioritize which decision-making criteria can only be investigated and identified through empirical research within a decision-theoretical approach. A criterion of functionality is an explanatory factor only when it is used as a decision-making criterion by political decision makers.

This chapter indicates that Stangl's basic hypothesis finds partial support. Party politicians do orient their decision making toward the interests of powerful clienteles, that is, they do follow a power max-imizing strategy. This, however, only holds for highly politicized issues. In cases of less politicized but nevertheless consequential decisions, conflict lines separate different sectors (e.g., justice versus economics) rather than political parties.

From the Justice Department to the Legislature

The federal government made prompt and intensive use of the sugges-tions developed by the expert commission. Already, parallel to the commission's work, it was drafting the First Law Against Economic Crime. This law went into effect on September 1, 1976, putting many of the commission's recommendations into practice. It included new proposals for offenses such as subsidy fraud (para. 264 *StGB*) and credit fraud. With this legislation, evidence of incorrect information given by borrowers constitutes an offense, even if harm has not (yet) been caused. Bankruptcy regulations were reintroduced into the criminal code, and usury was redefined in a comprehensive provision (para. 302a *StGB*).

Legislation for the Second Law was initiated soon after the commis-sion completed its work in 1975. Yet this process developed very hesi-tantly, for three reasons. First, it involved the highly controversial antitrust issue. Second, a large number of rather diverse offenses were included in the bill. Third, the political motivation to get tough on en-trepreneurs and white-collar offenders declined during the late 1970s. The liberal movement of the 1960s had faded and the economy had been troubled ever since the "oil shock" of 1973.

Our analysis of the legislative process is based on (1) content analysis of legislative documents, minutes of the judicial, budget, domestic affairs, and labor and welfare committees of the *Bundestag*; (2) intervi-ews with leading SPD and CDU/CSU representatives and with at-torneys of the federal and the Hesse departments of justice; (3) obse-rvation of a public hearing of the judicial committee; and, finally, (4) an analysis of the files of the German Federation of Industry (*Bund der Deutschen Industrie*, BDI) and interviews with numerous lobbyists.

We first give an overview of the legislative process, which, in its basic structure, is typical for German criminal justice legislation. We then give a detailed account of the administrative production of the bill and the efforts of lobbying groups to influence the process. Finally, we present an overview of the parliamentary process and describe the outcome of the legislation.

The Legislative Process

Lawyers of the Federal Department of Justice wrote a first draft of the Second Law in 1978 (see Figure 1, p. 6). This draft was presented to the state departments of justice who were asked for their input. Based on their reactions, the draft was modified. This method aims at securing political support in the *Bundesrat*, the state chamber, whose members are not elected legislators but representatives of the *Länder* (state) administrations. Yet difficulties and controversies over the bid rigging provision delayed the process. Only four years later, on April 6, 1982, did the SPD/FDP administration submit its bill to the *Bundesrat*. The purpose was "to continue the reform which began with the First Law Against Economic Crime. Additional changes in criminal and regulatory law ought to support the fight against economic crime" (Bundesregierung, Bundesrats-Drucksache 219/82 of June 4, 1982, p. 1). Means toward this end included the criminalization of computer fraud, the manipulation of computerized data, capital investment fraud, and several insurance-related offenses. In addition, the liability of corporate actors was to be increased.

The *Bundesrat* debated the bill, especially in its committees on the judiciary, interior, economics, and labor and welfare. Several of the committees suggested minor changes of particular proposals, which were decided on in a plenary session on July 16, 1982 and returned to the administration (Bundestags-Drucksache 219/82 of July 16, 1982). On September 30, 1982 the administration passed this bill, including the *Bundesrat*'s suggestions and its response to the *Bundestag* (Bundestags-Drucksache 9/2008 of September 30, 1982).

Legislative proposals die with the end of an administration. The administration changed in October 1982 when the libertarian coalition partner (FDP) left the SPD/FDP coalition led by Chancellor Helmut Schmidt, and joined ranks with the Christian Democrats. New elections in March 1983 brought a majority for the new CDU/CSU/FDP coalition and confirmed Chancellor Helmut Kohl's administration. Soon after the change of political majorities, on April 8, 1983, the new administration reinitiated the legislative process for the Second Law, aiming at the introduction or reform of the same 40 proposals included in the original bill. It passed this bill, originally developed in the social democratic administered justice department of the previous administration, to the *Bundesrat*. On April 29, 1983, the *Bundesrat* confirmed its decision of July 1982 to support this bill with minor modifications (Bundesrats-Drucksache 150/83).

Up to this point, the new political majorities had not changed the legislative process. Yet, the Social Democrats, now in the opposition, had become independent of their former coalition partner. They undertook several attempts to modify the legislative proposal. On May 13, 1983, the State of Hesse introduced an alternative bill into the *Bundesrat* (Land Hessen, Bundesrats-Drucksache 215/83), adding two new components to the old bill: the criminalization of bid rigging and of immoral employment practices. While the bid rigging proposal was supported by the judicial committee, the committees on the economy and on labor and welfare rejected the alternative bill. On July 1, 1983 the *Bundesrat* voted it down.

The second attempt to change the bill was initiated by a group of eleven SPD representatives in the *Bundestag* (equivalent to the U.S. House of Representatives). On June 8, 1983 they introduced a modified bill that included the criminalization of bid rigging and certain forms of labor subcontracting (Bundestags-Drucksache 10/119). Both the administration's bill and the SPD bill were debated in the House and passed on to the judiciary, interior, budget, economic affairs, and labor and welfare committees. The committee work began in November. On March 14, 1984 the committee on the judiciary supported the suggestion of its leading SPD member to hold a hearing on the issues of bid rigging, illegal subcontracting, and computer crime. This hearing was conducted in Bonn on June 6, 1984 (see Chapter 4). After these hearings the judicial committee did not debate the bills for a whole year. Only after the summer of 1985 did the committees return to the economic crime bills. In March 1986 the House resumed its plenary debate in its second and third session. The administration bill was passed in a modified form, but without a provision on bid rigging, and the law went into effect on August 1, 1986.

The long duration of the legislative process, even in its last stages, contrasted with expectations of leading participants. In an interview of February 1984, the leading CDU/CSU representative stated: "Passing the law should go rather speedily now. The judicial committee should be done by late March or early April. The House will probably pass the bill before summer 1984." The SPD speaker said, also in an interview of February 1984: "By March we will decide on the hearing. After the next committee session the bill should reenter the plenary session in April or May and be passed by the House before the summer recess." The attorneys in the Federal and Hesse Departments of Justice were more cautious and predicted the bill to pass late in 1984. We thus are confronted with considerable and unusual delays of the legislative process in both phases, the administrative drafting of the original bill and parliamentary decision making. The fight of business and industry associations was a major contributor to this delay.

The Ministerial Phase

The first draft of the Second Law Against Economic Crime, dated October 20, 1978, had been developed by lawyers of the Federal Department of Justice. It was strongly based on the commission's suggestions and included the criminalization of bid rigging behavior. This draft was forwarded to the state ministries of justice who passed it on to their prosecutors' offices and courts with a request for comments. The state ministries of justice summarized these comments and incorporated them in their response to the federal department. This process was completed by a conference of several days at which representatives of the state and federal justice departments participated. This "vertical" negotiation within the justice sector was complemented by "horizontal" coordination between different departments within the federal government. The result of these deliberations was the second draft of the bill of August 30, 1979, which continued to include the bid rigging proposal. We present several features characteristic of the whole process, before proceeding with a detailed account of its different phases.

First, all interviewees confirmed that the dispute over bid rigging offenses was the most difficult aspect of this process. They considered this dispute to be primarily responsible for the long period of four years it had taken to pass the ministerial draft by the cabinet and to hand it into the parliamentary process.

Second, the chief opponents in this dispute within the administration were the ministries of justice and of economic affairs. Opinions within the judicial sector had been almost unanimous, between the states and the federal government and among the different states, independent of their political majorities. Relations between liberal Hesse and conservative Bavaria and Baden-Württemberg had been extremely cooperative. Such cooperation was limited only when ministry attorneys had specific directives from their political superiors. For example, the attorney of the Baden-Württemberg department of justice refused any cooperation on the issue of bid rigging, referring explicitly to the interests of middle-class industry in his state.

In general though, the interstate and state-federal cooperation was characterized by intrasectoral harmony and intersectoral conflict, throughout the ministerial phase and independently of party-political constellations. One important specification must be made for the conflict between the justice and economics departments on the federal level. Here the intersectoral conflict became increasingly tense as interparty relations between the coalition partners deteriorated: the SPD controlled the justice department while the FDP controlled the department for economic affairs. In this conflict, sector-specific reasonings became confounded with class-specific interests. The constituency of the SPD is working class, that of the FDP includes many of the self-employed.

Third, throughout the process, industrial lobbying groups played a major role and contributed to the defeat first of antitrust proposals and, finally, of the remaining bid-rigging proposal.

The Industrial Lobby and Criminal Justice Legislation by Peter Brühl

These efforts of the industrial lobby are of central relevance for the legislative process. They can be broken down into four phases, which we describe in the following sections: (1) from the suggestions of the expert commission (1975) to the first ministerial draft of October 10, 1978; (2) from the first draft to the redefinition of the bid rigging provision of July 17, 1979; (3) from here to the second ministerial draft of 1980; (4) from the second draft to the administration's bill of June 2, 1982.

A central actor in this process was the German Federation of Industry (BDI), an umbrella organization for a diversity of sector specific industry associations (e.g., metal, chemical, construction). Headquartered in Cologne, its administration is organized along departmental lines (e.g., legal affairs, economic systems). Departments are linked with committees of the same specialty area. While departments are staffed with employees, committees are composed of representatives of different industries. In addition, specific working groups deal with more particular issues of more temporary relevance.

The main function of the BDI is to represent industry interests to the political sector and to coordinate actions taken by individual industries. The lobbying efforts against trust control legislation are one example. We were able to get access to the archives and to reconstruct systematically the industry's efforts to defeat this legislation, which industry perceived as a direct threat to some of its members and as a challenge to its own standing in society and toward the political sector. The following sections are a detailed account of the steps taken by the industrial sector.

Toward the First Ministerial Draft of the Second Law: The Files of the German Federation of Industry

This first of four phases during which industry lobbied the administration can itself be conveniently distinguished by three subphases:

from a first contact with the minister of justice on the trust control issue, to the construction of a coalition and preparatory steps, to, finally, a well orchestrated fight.

1. *The visit of the Federal Minister of Justice to the BDI Committee for Legal Affairs.* In 1975, the legal affairs committee invited the Federal Minister of Justice to present a lecture on the government's current legal policies. The minister accepted this invitation and a date was set for November 21, 1975. Dr. L suggested in letters of October 15 and 22 to prepare the meeting with the minister in such a way that the minister would face specific questions asked by selected committee members. On October 30, Dr. L received a draft of the minister's speech from an unnamed source. He distributed this draft to the chair and associate chair of the legal committee and proposed to discuss the questions to be directed at the minister in a meeting on November 10. Seven days later Dr. L sent additional materials to the committee chair. In an item on economic crime Dr. L proposed:

We should comment on the recommendations of the Commission for the Fight Against Economic Crime, which proposes to transform administrative antitrust offenses into criminal offenses.

Also on November 10, Dr. L sent a letter to an executive of a large oil corporation and member of the legal affairs committee to suggest critical questions concerning the criminalization of antitrust offenses.

On November 21, 1975, the *BDI* legal affairs committee held its fall meeting in Bonn. Item 1 was the preparation for the debate with the Minister of Justice. The members agreed on the questions that specific members would raise. The minister arrived at 11:30 a.m. to present his lecture (the first draft of which was already known to the committee members). Yet only some of the questions could be asked in the subsequent debate. The meeting was followed by a lunch and the minister was expected back at his department by 1:30 pm. The committee decided to mail the remaining questions to the minister, which was done on December 10. One of these questions asked whether newspaper reports in *Die Welt* and *Blick durch die Wirtschaft* of November 11, 1975 were correct, according to which the Minister of Justice deemed the criminalization of serious antitrust offenses unavoidable.

At a meeting of December 10, the *BDI* Department for Economic Systems informed its working group on antitrust issues of these activities and the letter to the Minister of Justice. While this information initiated little debate during the meeting, attorney R of the association of construction firms protested against the letter in a December 15 phone call to Dr. L. He considered it "dangerous at this time" and requested that the letter to the minister be stopped, especially for the sake of the Minister for Economic Affairs. Asking the Minister of Justice to determine his position now is really bad.

Yet the central office of the Federation had to inform the Construction Industry that the letter had already been mailed (letter of December 16), adding that Dr. Di, chief administrator of the Ministry for Economic Affairs, had expressed his concerns toward the Ministry of Justice. Two days later, Dr. M from the Department for Economic Systems provided additional information in a letter to the construction industry, that:

around December 10, 1975, state secretary Dr. Di of the Federal Department of Economic Affairs asked the Minister of Justice, explicitly in the name of his minister, not to follow the suggestions of the commission against economic crime and he requested information about the justice minister's opinion. . . . The minister will thus have to respond to the antitrust question anyway. Also, it is better if we animate the minister to respond than to have *Vorwärts* [a member magazine of the Social Democratic Party] or *Panorama* [a liberal magazine on national television] get ahead of us.

At its next meeting of January 26, 1976, the working group on antitrust law reconvened. Its members were now informed that the Department of Economic Affairs had officially intervened and expressed its opposition to the antitrust provisions. Further,

the Justice Department intends to first submit the draft to the interested associations and groups. It is still uncertain though if the department will then take a supportive stance.

The Department of Justice responded to the November questions in a letter of March 3, 1976. This letter did not contain a firm commitment on antitrust issues.

Given the responsibilities of different departments, the Minister for Economic Affairs will judge the proposal from an economic and antitrust perspective while my department will evaluate it from a legal policy perspective.

Yet the letter continued to say that the commission's proposals were "not unreasonable" from a legal policy perspective. Finally he argued that a hearing with the participation of business associations might be necessary before the final determinations of the administration. In a letter of March 16, 1976 the BDI Department for Economic Systems commented that the outcome of this issue will be determined by the separation of responsibilities between the ministries.

2. *The industry associations get ready.* The BDI working group on

antitrust policy started to debate strategies against the criminalization
of antitrust offenses at its meeting of December 10, 1975. Its members
considered this topic to be "most urgent" and suggested that an open
attack should be developed from that point on. They agreed that a
victory could only be gained in the early stages of the political process.
Contacts should therefore be sought at the highest levels. Further
issues concerned a public debate of the issue at one of the research
institutes of the economic sector; the alternative strategies of plain
resistance or cooperation toward a "reasonable" outcome; and the
commission of favorable expert opinions from selected jurisprudents.
Since no agreement could be reached, a new meeting date was set for
January 26. This time it was agreed that

given the dangers political opportunists may cause in a public debate, every-
thing must be avoided that could lead to force proponents of criminalizations
into the open.

The following steps ought to be taken: (a) collecting arguments
against the proposal; (b) documenting the particularities of U.S. antitrust law and its relation to German law, based on a report of the Association of Chemical Industries and further developed in collaboration
with lawyers who represented German corporations in the United
States; (c) commissioning an expert opinion on the French situation
with a French expert; and (d) commissioning an expert opinion with a
German jurisprudent on the proposal of the Commission Against
Economic Crime which would also consider constitutional concerns.
     Material on item (b) was contributed in subsequent weeks by the
Association of Chemical Industry and lawyers of Bayer and Esso Corporations, the latter in collaboration with an executive of Exxon (New
York). A BDI lawyer used these documents to compose a comprehensive report on the situation of American antitrust law. On September 16, 1976, the Department for Economic Systems sent two reports
on the American and French experiences to the working group on
antitrust law, noting:

Our research on the American situation does not yield results in support of our
position. . . . Yet, it seems to be useful to argue with regard to the French
experience.

First initiatives toward strategy (d), the commission of an expert
opinion with a German jurisprudent, are documented in the files of
July 1976. On July 13, the chair of the BDI Department for Economic
Systems met with Professor I (University W) to explore whether "[I]
could write an expert opinion on the criminalization of antitrust law."

Professor I had earlier attracted the attention of organized business when he had given critical testimony against the First Law Against Economic Crime before the *Bundestag* Special Committee on Criminal Law. Yet the conversation did not result in collaboration. While the scholar agreed that a criminalization of antitrust offenses could result in unfair treatment of firms, he also showed some sympathy with Professor T and his work with the Commission Against Economic Crime. The lobbyist and the professor agreed to stay in touch and to consider I as a presenter should the Research Institute of German Industry (*FIW*) decide for a conference on the issues involved.

3. *Counter-measures of the industry associations*. On August 26, 1976 an important event resulted in much more decisive and speedy action of the industrial lobby. The Justice Department officially sent the proposals from the tenth meeting of the Commission Against Economic Crime to the industry associations, requesting written responses by November 15. Industry immediately initiated three strategies: (a) preparation of written comments for the Justice Department; (b) commissioning a jurisprudential expert opinion; and (c) initiating contacts with decision makers in both chambers of the legislature.

(a) On November 14, 1976, the BDI Department for Economic Systems informed its committee and the member associations that it planned a thorough response to the Justice Department's request.

We suggest that you either give your own response . . . or support the response of the Industry Federation. . . . Should you give your own response to the Justice Department at an earlier date, please send us a copy.

In a letter of November 24 the Department for Economic Systems informed the Federation members that it planned to coordinate its response with the German Federation of Chambers of Commerce (*Deutscher Industrie und Handelstag*). Both federations, in collaboration with the Association of Construction Industries, convinced the Justice Department to postpone the deadline to the end of the year. Between October 21 and November 22, fourteen business associations responded to the Federation's request. Copies of three more papers which had been sent directly to the Justice Department arrived by December 21. On November 25 and December 2 the Department for Economic Systems sent two parts of a draft response to its committee for discussions in meetings of December 1 and 29 in which eight business associations participated (six of which had not previously participated). Thus 23 different industry associations participated in this action. The joint statement was sent out by the BDI on January 4, 1977. In addition, on January 6, 1977, the Federation of Chambers of Commerce delivered its own testimony to the Justice Department with signatures of sixteen of its member associations. In sum, a powerful and highly activated business response attacked the criminalization proposals of the Commission Against Economic Crime, especially as they related to antitrust offenses.

(b) The search for jurisprudential expertise proved difficult. In a letter of September 16, 1976 the BDI Department of Economic Systems informed its members that no scholar in the area of criminal law could be found for a commissioned expert opinion. The vast majority backed the suggestions of the Economic Crime Commission. Yet success was achieved in late September. A note from September 24, 1976, indicates that two constitutional lawyers, professors K and J, might be suited to write the paper. While parallel explorations were conducted with three other scholars, agreement was soon reached with Professor K. A lawyer of Esso Corporation had first met with K on September 30, and delivered BDI documents. A second, more thorough conversation including a BDI representative and Professor K was conducted on October 15 in the office of the corporate lawyer. The price for the expert opinion was set at 30,000 German marks, which is "quite normal for an 80-page paper; nothing could be negotiated down" (BDI files). There are some indications that, after written communications in November and December, another meeting took place on December 10, 1976 in the Esso headquarters to debate a first draft of K's paper. The Federation added a summary of K's constitutional arguments against the commission's proposals to its response to the Justice Department on January 4, 1977.

(c) On September 30, 1976 the BDI Department for Economic Systems sent a letter to the Bavarian Minister for Economic Affairs, whose critical position toward the commission's proposals had become known earlier. On October 5 the Ministry wrote back, enclosing a copy of its own critical response to the Justice Department from February 1976. A new ally had been gained with considerable weight in the state chamber of the federal legislature.

The BDI further contacted a *Bundestag* representative who chaired the FDP working group for economic affairs, thus reaching out to the small libertarian coalition party. The Federation contacted an influential conservative representative from the Bavarian CSU party who, "of course," was opposed to the commission's proposals (BDI file, December 2, 1976). It was agreed that the two sides would meet in early 1977 to discuss the issues further. One of the BDI's chief managers now decided to send copies of Professor K's expert opinion to these two representatives and to the secretary of the CDU, the main opposition party. It was also decided not to contact any representative of the Social Democrats so as not to provoke any counterproductive action. Very few additional communications are documented in the *BDI* files for the rest of 1977 and 1978.

On October 20, 1978, the Justice Department presented its "Ministerial Draft of a Second Law Against Economic Crime." Only one of the commission's proposals to criminalize antitrust offenses had survived, the proposal against bid rigging (paragraph 264a *Strafgesetzbuch-Referentenentwurf*). This proposal aimed at criminalizing attempts to make or initiate flawed bids.

From the First Ministerial Draft to the Reformulation of the Proposal Against Bid Rigging of July 17, 1979

At this stage of the process responsibility within the BDI moved from the Department for Economic Systems to the Department for Legal Affairs. The latter sent the Justice Department's proposal to its Committee, its Working Group on Criminal Code Reform, and the Federation's member associations (letter of December 22, 1978). On January 5, 1979, a high representative of the Association of Construction Firms called the Federation and argued that

a working group of concerned industries ought to be created to debate strategies against the ministerial proposal. Paragraph 264a must be eliminated at all costs. . . . No time must be lost.

The construction industry was informed that no other response had been received by the BDI (letter of January 24, 1979). Yet, in a letter of February 1, the legal affairs department invited those addressed in the December letter to meet for a discussion of the ministry's proposal.

Prior to this talk, on February 12, a leading representative of the construction association (W) met with experts from the federal Departments for Justice (B) and Economic Affairs (D). Especially the meeting with D proved to be important. D pointed out, according to W,

that it is absolutely necessary that we coordinate the proceedings with the Industry Federation and with other leading industry associations. We should not argue with the specific conditions of our industry but develop a strategy against the proposed entry into the criminalization of antitrust law in co-ordination with all industries. . . . The Ministry for Economic Affairs will give its own response to the Justice Department by March 15. By then our position and that of the Industry Federation should have been communicated to the Ministry.

W asked the BDI on February 20 to pressure other leading associations to join in the protest. On March 1, 1979, the Association of Construction Industries sent its extensive comments to the Ministries of Justice and Economic Affairs. The other leading umbrella organizations sent their comments on March 29.

On July 17, 1979 the Justice Department presented a revised and more lenient version of paragraph 264a. This version no longer criminalized attempts to engage other competitors in flawed bids. Only the actual making of such bids remained in the proposal. The industry associations had achieved another partial success.

Toward the Final Ministry Proposal

The new proposal initiated a new wave of activities in the industrial sector. The Association of Construction Industries sent a copy of the proposal to the Industry Federation (BDI, November 19, 1979), responded with its own critique to the Justice Department (November 26), and pleaded to the Honorary President and Vice President of the Industry Federation (V) (December 10). In the December letter the President of the Association of Construction Industries asked V to raise the issue

resolutely with the presiding board of the Industry Federation and to plea that the Federation's president present the critical opinion of industry to the concerned ministries, especially the Ministry of Justice.

The Association of Construction Industries and the Industry Federation exchanged several additional messages. The essential point, however, is documented in a note in the BDI files (January 22, 1980).

Unfortunately the other member associations have not indicated any interest in further initiatives, assuming that they had been saved after the antitrust initiative was reduced to bid rigging offenses. This might prove to be a mistake. . . . The member associations should turn their attention to ongoing developments and fully support our resistance.

Yet by the end of May only three industry associations and the construction industry had participated in the Federation's initiative against the bid rigging provision.

On June 18, 1980 a meeting at BDI headquarters took place, requested by the President of the Construction Industry (X). Participants were, in addition to X, two other lobbyists for the Construction Industries (Y and U) and the Chair of the BDI Committee for Economic Systems (Q). X regretted, according to a Federation memo, that "the majority of Industry Associations are uninterested. . . . He [X] had talked himself to the Ministers B, C, and (recently) D." X now demanded an intensified political involvement of the *BDI*. "X expects that now the BDI opposes, on its highest level, the inclusion of paragraph

264a cabinet proposal." M of the Federation pointed out that "political involvement of the BDI on the highest level requires strong consensus of our members on the ultimate importance of the issue. . . . It would be required that the issue be debated by the chief executives of our member associations. X will send a written request to the BDI." This request was never received by the BDI (note of November 12, 1980).

This third phase of the administrative process came to an end when the Justice Department submitted its reformulated proposal of the entire bill. This proposal continued to include the second draft of the proposal against bid rigging.

From the Ministry Proposal to the Cabinet Proposal of June 2, 1982

The final phase of the administration's work had come. On October 29, 1980, the BDI legal affairs department sent the draft of a new response to the Justice Department's proposal to other umbrella organizations of the economy. The final version of this statement went out to federal departments, including the Justice Department, on November 24, 1980. It, again, dealt critically with the bid rigging provision.

Only the construction industry opposed this procedure. Yet, the Industry Federation was sceptical about its suggestion to approach the ministers directly and personally. They were especially reluctant to do so, as an internal Federation memo states, "since the chances to change the minister's [of justice] mind are practically zero." Even so, the principal officer of the construction lobby argued:

I think it is useful to await the new legislative period to examine if the Justice Department will continue to pursue its goals against the resistance of the department for economic affairs. We should then decide at a more appropriate time if conversations with the ministers are appropriate.

Letters in support of the Construction Industries position arrived from the Association for Steel Construction and Energy Techniques and from the Association for Machine Production. The BDI office then responded in a letter of December 8, 1980 that its President intended to "also raise this issue in his upcoming personal meeting with the federal minister for economic affairs on urgent issues." A BDI memo preparing for this meeting (no date, no signature) states: "[Minister for Economic Affairs] should be encouraged to hold onto his resistance, also vis-à-vis the Justice Minister." The meeting between the BDI president and the Federal Minister of Economic Affairs, in which only the Federation's chief administrator participated, was held on December 12, 1980.

After a considerable gap and new federal elections, which resulted in the same SPD/FDP coalition government with a new Minister of Justice, the cabinet finally decided on the Second Law Against Economic Crime on June 2, 1982. The bid rigging provision was not included. All antitrust provisions had been successfully rejected when the suggestions of the expert commission were transformed into the administration's bill. The bill was now passed on to the *Bundestag*.

Industry and the Executive Branch: Preliminary Conclusions
by Peter Brühl

The process of lobbying in the first phase differed considerably from that in phases two to four. During the first phase the Justice Department tended toward a rather broad attack on deviant entrepreneurs through the criminalization of several antitrust offenses, following the commission's recommendation. Industry took this plan very seriously. After the Lawyers Association meetings at the beginning of the commission's work had not motivated a strong participation of the industrial lobby, and after industry had found rather limited access to the commission's work, many associations and corporations now entered collective action, guided by the BDI. The strong mobilization during these later phases was successful. Only the bid rigging provision survived.

After the defeat of a broad criminalization of antitrust offenses, major portions of industry lost interest and the fight was carried on by the Association of Construction Industries in cooperation with the BDI. The Federation was not inclined to take major steps that would not be supported by some of its major member associations. It resisted the construction industry's pressure to initiate personal meetings with the concerned ministries on the highest level. Yet a compromise strategy appeared toward the end of the process. While a meeting with the Justice Minister did not seem to promise any success, the president of the Industry Federation agreed to include the bid rigging issue in his proposed meeting with the Minister for Economic Affairs.

The following preliminary conclusions can be drawn and supported by additional evidence.

1. Economic associations and corporations get involved in massive lobbying efforts when their interests are threatened by the drafting of criminal law bills in the federal administration.

2. Economic associations and corporations cease or diminish their lobbying efforts when only particular branches of the economy are threatened by such legislation.

3. The massive mobilization of industry leads to success in the fight against criminalizing norms.

4. Isolated branches of industry that perceive their particular inter-

ests to be threatened through economic crime legislation try to mobilize industrial umbrella organizations to improve their chances.

5. The influence of industry associations on the Justice Department, characterized by sectoral antagonism, is more limited than on the Economic Affairs Department, characterized by sectoral empathy.

6. Influence on the Economic Affairs Department is even stronger when the department's leadership holds close ties to industry, which is typically the case.

The latter factor weighed especially in the given case and requires some additional information. The Justice Minister was a Social Democrat. The Economic Affairs Minister (D) was a member of the libertarian Free Democrats. (D) had declared his opposition to such proposals even before he joined the cabinet. In 1975 he was a member of the *Bundestag* and his faction's speaker on economic issues. Asked about the criminalization of antitrust offenses at a meeting at the Industry Research Institute (*Forschungsinstitut für Wirtschaftsverfassung und Wettbewerb*) in November 1975 he "responded in front of the whole assembly that he would not participate in the nonsense of a criminalization of antitrust offenses" (letter from Dr. M [BDI] to Dr. W [Aral Corporation] from November 17, 1975). Representative D stayed in close touch on this issue with the industry association throughout the following years (e.g., phone conversation with the BDI chief administrator in November 1976; letter from January 1977). After D became Minister for Economic Affairs in October 1977, contact continued. A high-level lawyer of the Economics Department met with a lawyer from the construction lobby on February 2, 1979 and suggested that the lobbying organization

should address the minister again. . . . The ministry attempts to delay the legislation beyond this legislative period and possibly to prevent it.

Some 14 months later, after the bid rigging provision had been revised, the president of the construction lobby met with the minister (April 21, 1980). At the June 18 meeting with members of the BDI he reported that "(D) is strictly against this provision and may use this issue to break the coalition [with the Social Democrats in the Schmidt administration]." This remark of (D) was thus known to the BDI when its president raised the bid rigging issue in his meeting with the minister on December 12, 1980. It is not known but likely that the Industry Federation encouraged the strategy the minister had proposed earlier in the year.

We do not know whether the minister actually threatened to break the coalition in the decisive cabinet meeting of June 2, 1982. At any rate, the bid rigging provision was eliminated at this point, and it is very unlikely that the Justice Department would have changed its mind at this late point in the process. On September 17, 1982 the coalition broke up when the Free Democrats pulled out. It was soon replaced by a CDU/CSU/FDP coalition under Chancellor Kohl. Minister (D) played a major role in this break-up by making numerous "provocative comments in interviews" (*Der Spiegel*, No. 37, September 13, 1982), opposing the economic policy directive of his administration. No FDP member pushed this defeat as strongly as (D), the "*Königsmörder*"[1] (*Der Spiegel*, No. 38, September 20, 1982, pp. 17–18).

In sum, two different philosophies on the role of the economy clashed: the social democratic understanding of the economy as a servant of society, to be reprimanded when deviant, versus the libertarian philosophy that suggests a much higher degree of freedom for entrepreneurial behavior even if this implies the acceptance of deviance. Each philosophy has its own implications for criminal justice. After fourteen years of promoting the social democratic view under the Brandt and Schmidt administrations, the conservative side regained power and the attempted criminalization of entrepreneurial behavior was defeated.

Economic rationales and industrial power potentials invaded and overcame a concept of criminal guilt that had been unanimously proposed by the criminal justice sector, including criminal jurisprudents, criminal law practitioners, and justice departments. Yet it was not abstract or systemic economic interests that prevailed in this case, but the interests of concrete actors, possibly against the abstract functional requirements of an industry that was badly adapted to given market structures (see Chapter 4). This suggests that concrete class interests can defeat notions of justice under the disguise of sector rationalities even when they are in fact opposed to those rationalities. Stangl is right, at least for the antitrust and bid rigging proposals, when he hypothesizes that policy issues (here justice policy, perhaps even economic policy) get reformulated into political issues (power) in political decision-making processes.

Parliamentary Decision Makers: Deliberations in the Judicial Committee of the *Bundestag*

No matter what groups try to influence law making and what functions may be anticipated or fulfilled by the laws, decisions about laws are made in the political system. In the German political system, especially

1. *Königsmörder* (emperor's murderer) is a German idiom referring to someone who defeats one's own leader, often to increase one's own power base.

as compared to that of the United States, the administration is much more powerful than the parliament because of its more plentiful resources and its specialists. The proposal for the Second Law Against Economic Crime was written by the Department of Justice, assisted by the commission and the Departments of Justice of the Federal States. Yet the final decision in law making always has to be made by the parliament. Parliament positions and majorities are anticipated by the administration when it prepares a law. The independent impact of parliament also showed in our case when several changes in the administration's draft were made during the legislative process.

It is therefore worthwhile to look at the parliament's role. After a first and rather short plenary session, the bill was passed on to the committees for detailed discussion. Because this was a criminal law proposal, the judicial committee was dominant and formally responsible. It negotiated on all paragraphs of the proposed law, whereas the other committees involved (domestic, economics, budget, labor, and social affairs) discussed only particular aspects. In the end, the judicial committee had to gather the statements of all others and give recommendations to the parliament for the final plenary session. It was in the judiciary, therefore, where the specialists of the different factions negotiated and prepared the final decisions. However, time is very limited in the judicial committee, and its debates rather restricted. The criminalization of bid rigging, the most disputed paragraph in the law, was discussed only once and then for about one hour (not counting the public hearing held by the judicial committee, mentioned above). Perhaps the unwillingness of the opposing parties to compromise on this issue contributed to the brevity of the discussion. This one hour did not include all the negotiations on this point. Instead, the positions expressed there had been reached through long negotiations within intraparty work groups where representatives of different parties had informally discussed the issue. The debate in the judicial committee thus reflected much more than just one moment of parliamentary work.

We analyzed the structures of the actors' lines of argument during this session of the judicial committee to identify their motives and underlying political interests and rationalities. For this purpose we again used the cognitive mapping approach (see Chapters 1 and 3 above).

Argumentation in the Judicial Committee. The document analyzed in this section is the minutes of the session of the judicial committee of the *Bundestag* on the criminalization of bid rigging held on November 24, 1983 (for the relevance of this meeting, see above). About fifty persons were present, and eight participated in the debate. Before proceeding

TABLE 9. Distribution of Concepts Used by Types of Decision Makers and Social Spheres (target concepts in parentheses)

| Type of decision maker | Concept by social sphere | | | |
	Economy	Legitimation	Criminal law	Total
SPD representative	2 (1)	1 (1)	8 (3)	11 (5)
Speaker for the Department of Justice in SPD-governed Hesse	2 (1)	0 (0)	11 (4)	13 (5)
CDU/CSU representative	10 (3)	0 (0)	4 (1)	14 (4)
Total	14 (5)	1 (1)	23 (8)	38 (14)

to the individual cognitive maps, we present an overview of the concepts that were used by different types of decision makers (see Table 9). The concepts are differentiated according to different social spheres, the decision makers according to their positions as representatives of the Social Democratic Party (SPD) or the Christian Democratic Union/Christian Social Union (CDU/CSU). The representative of the Department of Justice of Hessen, an SPD-governed state that had earlier tried to criminalize price fixing through the state chamber, represents the third type of speaker. With the exception of one concept relating to legitimation ("I1: astonishment of citizens," see Figure 10), the others may be categorized as related to the economy or criminal law.

Among the economic concepts are A2 (quota of firm-owned capital), D5 (damage through bankruptcies), and D2 (development of damages). Legal concepts include C1 (feeling of guilt), F3 (helplessness of the criminal justice system), and H2 (violation of the principle of legal equality). It is not surprising that in the judicial committee the majority of concepts relate to legal policy (23 concepts), although the economic sector apparently also plays a major role (14 concepts).

A comparison of different types of decision makers is illuminating. Among the concepts used by SPD representatives, some 20 percent were economic and 10 percent referred to legitimation, but more than 70 percent were law and criminal policy concepts. There was even more stress on legal concepts by the speaker for the Hesse Department of Justice. The relation between different types of concepts is just the opposite for the CDU/CSU representatives. In this debate of the judicial committee on a criminal law norm, they used more than twice as many economic concepts as legal ones. Even if this categorization of concepts is rough, and even if nothing is yet said on the direction of the arguments, our data certainly support Schick's (1981) hypothesis that conflicts between purposes of criminal policy and regulatory needs of noncriminal law fields are more likely to occur in the *Nebenstrafrecht* (criminal law provisions that refer to specific areas of regulation such as environment and economy and are not part of the Criminal Code) than in the general Criminal Code. It also supports Weber's (1978, pp. 880–889) prognosis that increasing particularization of law will be accompanied by an invasion of substantive rationalities from nonlegal spheres into the legal discourse that intrudes into its formal rationality.

To understand the decision makers' arguments more precisely, it is necessary to have a closer look at their cognitive maps, that is, all causal-argumentative contributions that were given in the case under investigation. Six speakers gave statements that reflected cognitive arguments: three CDU/CSU representatives, two SPD representatives, and the judge representing the Department of Justice of Hesse.

Let us first follow the contributions by the CDU/CSU representatives in the order in which they were presented. The first contribution contains the simple cognitive map of Representative B, the official speaker of his faction for this law. He first said that price fixing is a negative function of the volume of orders to firms. He explained the increase of such behavior in times of economic crisis and lack of orders, a situation that was particularly relevant for the construction industry. This speaker also saw a positive causal relation between the strength of sanctions or the degree of criminalization of price fixing and the frequency with which price fixing occurs. This implies the assumption of a general preventive effect of the proposed norm. Apparently he follows the economic model of the entrepreneurial offender. This argumentation per se would be opposed to the position of Representative B's party, which rejected the norm and instead supports the position of the SPD.

In an interview, this representative stated that he originally was not really opposed to this norm but that the economic wing of his political faction had made a strong argument against it. It had prevailed in the faction and he had to represent that position in the committee. His original stand is not so surprising if we consider that for quite a while he had been the mayor of a middle-sized town and as such had represented a typical victim of this type of price fixing. Nevertheless, his first argument modifies the second part of his statement. By explaining firms' deviations in terms of their miserable economic situation, Representative B follows an anomie approach, which is not at all typical for conservative representatives since such an argument usually favors aid programs rather than criminalizations. The contribution of this speaker was followed by those of the other decision makers. Only toward the end of the session did the other two CDU/CSU representa-

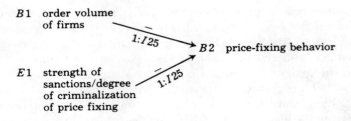

Figure 7. Cognitive map of Representative B (CDU/CSU) on
bid rigging.

tives further defend the position of their party. Their arguments were
almost exclusively economic.

The cognitive map of Representative C, which is shown in Figure 8,
contains neither the concept of price-fixing behavior nor that of the
proposed norm. Instead he discussed the problematic economic situation of the construction industry, including its conditions and impacts.
In the center of the argumentation we find the degree of cost coverage
of offers advertised by public investors. Representative C assumes that
the cost coverage is a function of the quota of capital that is owned by
the firm and of the "toughness" of public negotiators when contracts
between public authorities and private firms are worked out. This
"toughness" is explained through the presently small investment bud-
gets of municipalities, states, and the federal government. Considering
this situation and the presently low quota of firm-owned capital, one
must assume a low degree of cost coverage of offers. The results are a
high amount of necessary repairs (low cost coverage means badly
executed works) and a high rate of damage through bankruptcies.

Representative C does not make any direct statement on the (non)-
desirability of the proposed criminal law norm nor any criminal law or
legal policy argument at all. His opinions on these terms can be drawn
only if his contribution is seen in combination with that of his colleague, Representative B. If we combine the latter's deterrence hypothesis with Representative C's arguments, the criminal law norm
would result once more in a decreased degree of cost coverage due to a
further weakened position of the firms. The norm would finally result
in high damages through bankruptcies and in the increasing need for
repairs.

Cognitive maps were originally seen as representations of the knowledge of individuals, although I have modified this understanding. In
group discussions, these maps must certainly be interpreted in the
context of the argumentations of other participants. In this context,

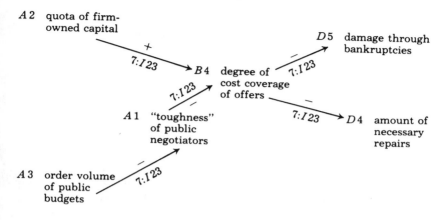

Figure 8. Cognitive map of Representative C (CDU/CSU) on bid rigging.

the next CDU/CSU speaker, Representative D, picks up the arguments of Representative C.

One could say that he leads them to their conclusions about criminal law policy (see Figure 9). According to this speaker, the low volume of firms' orders increases the number of price-fixing cases. Price-fixing behavior, after the introduction of the criminal law norm, would lead to criminal court cases in which the new norm would be applied. This would result in bankruptcies and layoffs of workers. This consequence might follow directly from sanctions against entrepreneurs. It might also, referring to the arguments of the other CDU/CSU speakers, stem from the deterrence effect and the resulting further decreasing profitability of firms. The line of arguments of the CDU/CSU representatives ends with the most effective economic concern against the criminal policy arguments of the Social Democratic speakers, particularly in times of economic crisis: the loss of jobs.

Certain conclusions may be drawn from this analysis of the cognitive maps of the CDU/CSU representatives. Their lines of argument were logically consistent, and they supported the position of their party by assuming that the criminalization of price fixing would have a deterrent effect. Despite (or because of) this, they opposed such criminalization, supporting their position mostly with economic arguments. The CDU/CSU representatives tried to explain price fixing through the difficult economic situation of entrepreneurs or their firms. They pointed to negative economic consequences that they expect from criminalization.

This argumentation differs from the pattern typically followed by

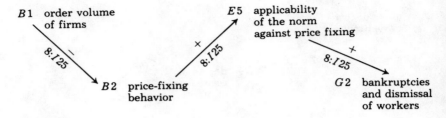

Figure 9. Cognitive map of Representative D (CDU/CSU) on bid rigging.

representatives of the conservative party in criminal law debates. They normally stress individual freedom and responsibility to act in one way or the other, consistent with or against existing norms. Consequently in other debates they agree with the criminal law principle of individual guilt. CDU Representative Gude, for example, expressed the following programmatic opinion on the general reform of the criminal code:

Scientific knowledge can no longer be directed against the demand that human beings must and should be addressed as moral persons by criminal law. . . . Who demands freedom for human beings must also load responsibility upon them. . . . This proposal bases criminal law on the idea of individual guilt. (Deutscher Bundestag 1963: 3193)

The comparison of this statement in a general debate on the criminal code, referring to "typical criminals," with the argumentations analyzed above, which refer to entrepreneurs' offenses, reveals one of the contradictions discussed earlier.

Before interpreting this contradiction, however, we shall discuss the argumentations of the SPD representatives. With Representative A (see Figure 10) we find two nonconnected lines of arguments. The target concept of the shorter line is the astonishment of citizens, said to be caused by the violation of the principle of equality. The speaker implied that the present law offered economic offenders lower chances than others to be sanctioned for acts that cause relatively high damage. Or, expressed in more sociological terms, the violation of the principle of equality caused a loss of legitimation (for the state and for the criminal justice system). This argument supported the SPD demand for the introduction of the proposed norm. The same holds true for the more complex line of arguments. The strategic variables of "broadness" of the norm and strength of sanctions/degree of criminalization introduced the causal chain. The argument claimed that a broadly formulated norm could help to overcome the existing helplessness of the criminal justice system and thereby to counteract, in combination

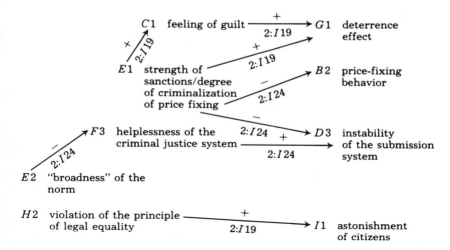

Figure 10. Cognitive map of Representative A (SPD) on bid rigging.

with severe sanctions, the present instability of the bidding system. Severe sanctions were assumed to increase the offenders' feeling of guilt and the deterrence effect and thereby directly to diminish price-fixing behavior. All of these arguments strongly supported the SPD position in favor of the criminalization of bid rigging. Representative A agreed with CDU/CSU Representative B that the norm would have deterrent effects, but unlike the CDU/CSU representatives did not discuss the conditions that cause this type of deviant behavior.

The contribution of Representative A was supported by that of his colleague Representative E (see Figure 11). According to Representative E, a criminal law norm for price fixing would have three effects: to diminish the helplessness of the criminal justice system, increase the deterrence effect, and limit the amount of damage caused by price fixing. This argumentation, like that of Representative A, supported the SPD position for the introduction of the norm.

In sum, the analysis of the argumentations of the SPD representatives yields the following conclusions. Like those of the CDU/CSU representatives, they are logically consistent and support the demands of their party. SPD representatives likewise believe in the deterrent effects of the criminalization of price fixing. For them, however, this supports the proposed norm. The SPD representatives, as opposed to those from the CDU/CSU, used predominantly legal policy arguments that mostly concern legal and criminal policy impacts of criminalization. These impacts were chiefly positively evaluated. SPD politi-

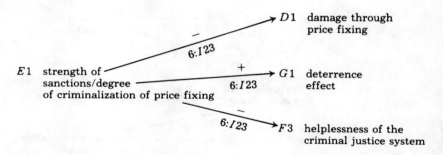

Figure 11. Cognitive map of Representative E (SPD) on bid rigging.

cians did not deal with the conditions of the problematized behavior. As is true of the CDU/CSU representatives, the orientation of their argumentations was exactly opposite to their typical position in criminal law debates. SPD politicians tend to stress the societal conditions of deviant behavior as well as the problematic impacts of criminalization. As SPD Representative Wittrock expressed in the session on the general criminal code reform mentioned above: "There are types of behavior that do not necessarily need to be sanctioned as this proposal does. . . . The demand for a minimal program of criminal law must be concluded from our position" (Deutscher Bundestag 1963, p. 3199).

The fact that conservative and social democratic politicians exchange their criminal policy roles when they deal with entrepreneurs as offenders, a group that is usually not an object of such debates, suggests that both political parties are inconsistent in their punitive or socio-political orientation. They use and exchange these orientations to serve their clienteles, protecting their own from sanctioning and threatening the clientele of the other party with sanctions. This certainly supports Haferkamp's (1980) understanding of criminal law policy as a dominance-group-related policy.

Two other observations allow conclusions that are characteristic for many parliamentary decision-making processes: (1) the lines of argument are extremely short; and (2) the speakers of the different factions present their positions without referring at all to those of the other side. Only one concept was used by both sides. This contradicts the widespread belief that in the West German political system the basic parliamentarian work is done in committees. What we observe instead is the use of relatively simple arguments to justify and legitimize decisions that had earlier been made within factions or party groups. This observation, however, cannot be generalized. When the judicial committee discussed computer crime, for example, members of the two factions cooperated closely and worked on the formulation of norms. Purely legitimation-oriented negotiation such as that seen in the price-fixing case seems to be likely when an issue is highly disputed between the parties and when the debate is polarized. The structures of the CDU/CSU representatives' arguments were still "shorter" and less complex than those of the SPD representatives. This confirms the findings of studies in decision theory that the argumentation of those decision makers who are in a minority position is more complex (Gallhofer and Saris 1984). Those who have power feel less need to exhaust themselves with long and complicated argumentations, which thus generates simpler cognitive maps.

We finally look briefly at the most complex contribution, offered by the speaker for the Hesse Department of Justice, X. Space does not allow us to present his cognitive maps and to discuss them in detail; they use twenty concepts and make fifteen causal assumptions within five different graphs. This can be explained by at least two factors. First, as a bureaucrat who is also a judge, he is a specialist in the issue under consideration, whereas the parliamentarians, as generalists, must always deal with a diversity of issues. Second, he argues for a minority position.

This speaker's argumentation supported the SPD demand for the introduction of the criminal provision against price fixing for two reasons. Speaker X argued for a SPD-governed state and as the speaker of the criminal justice system. His position can therefore be explained by the class-orientation thesis and by the systemic rationality of the law sector. In fact, fourteen of his fifteen arguments were expressed in terms of legal and criminal policy.

To legitimize his position Speaker X simultaneously used an etiological and a labeling argument. First he assumed an autonomous increase in economic crime. Then he attributed the increasing number of identified offenses to the growing activity of the prosecutors. This appears as a convenient although somewhat contradictory legitimation strategy for a control agency that aims to legitimize itself through a large number of identified deviations. At the same time it stresses the need for additional resources and personnel to meet the increasing pressure in terms of an actual increase in offenses.

The Outcome of the Legislation: Structure and Selection

The committee work was completed with the recommendation and final report of the judicial committee passed to the *Bundestag* on February 19, 1986 (Bundestagsdrucksache 10/5058). This report included the decisions of the judicial committee and proposed an extended and modified version of the administration's bill. This modified bill passed the *Bundestag* in March 1986 with the broad support of the factions of the conservative CDU/CSU, the social democratic SPD, and the libertarian FDP (with the Greens abstaining). Almost nobody wanted to be absent when white-collar offenders were criminalized. Those who had originally fought for the antitrust provisions no longer bound their support for the bill to a success in the antitrust area.

Having discussed the defeat of the anti-trust provisions in great detail we now summarize the other provisions of the bill and some transformations they underwent in the parliamentary phase. We organize these provisions into four sections: (1) provisions to ease the attribution of criminal liability in business organizations; (2) computer offenses; (3) capital investment offenses; and (4) others.

1. The original bill intended to extend criminal liability in firms to high-level employees who autonomously direct certain spheres of business activity (*Vertreterhaftung*; para. 14 II 1 *StGB*). This would have extended criminal liability for illegal business practices beyond the circle of business owners and would have allowed for many more successful prosecutions against organizational offenses. This provision had already created disputes in the *Bundesrat*, the state chamber. Strongly supported by the judicial committee, it was critically questioned by the committees for domestic and economic affairs. While the state chamber had voted for this proposal, following the judicial committee's recommendation, its opponents were partially victorious in the later stages of the parliamentary process. According to the final version, passed by the House, employees can only be criminally liable if they have been explicitly charged with taking on particular entrepreneurial functions. This restrictive wording of the provision continues to bar criminal law's application to most organizational offenses.

Two related provisions were introduced into the misdemeanor code. A juridical person or a corporate entity could now be fined for offenses even if illegal behavior could not be attributed to any particular individual or agent of that corporation (para. 30 *OWiG*). Furthermore causing harm and danger to employees and firms through offenses against organizational rules could now more easily result in misdemeanor charges against violators of supervisory duties than was previously the case (*Aufsichtspflichtverletzung*; para. 130 *OWiG*). The maximum fine for this offense was raised from 100,000 to 1,000,000 German marks. Both proposals were, however, weakened through modifications achieved by the CDU/CSU faction. These modifications render successful implementation of the provisions questionable, according to several speakers at the House (*Bundestag*) hearing.

2. The original bill proposed to criminalize several computer offenses. The provision of fraudulent behavior was reworded so that fraud resulting in harm to other people's property was also covered if it was achieved through the manipulation of computers (para. 263 *StGB*). Several manipulations were interpreted as equivalent to deceptive acts in traditional fraud: false programming, manipulation of the working of a program (through commands or manipulation of hardware), and the use of incorrect or incomplete data. If such manipulations influence the result of the computing process and harm others' property, they will be considered fraud. This proposal passed the state chamber without any debate. Following the hearings in the House, however, the provision was toughened. Now the use of other persons' code numbers and unauthorized access to others' videotexts was also included in the provision.

Another "computer provision" aims at the forgery of computed data, thus extending the traditional paragraph against the forgery of documents (para. 269 *StGB*). Electronic data are now considered documents if they would be considered as documents in a printed form. The punishment for the manipulation of such data would be up to five years imprisonment or fines. The state chamber, after initiatives of the committees for the judiciary and for economic and domestic affairs, voted to suggest a possible extension of this provision, which was eventually achieved in the House. Even unauthorized computer processing of document-type data is now covered by the provision.

Debates surrounding the *Bundestag* hearing on computer offenses resulted in further provisions which were also passed. Following suggestions by scholars and computer corporations, unauthorized access and spying on other persons' data banks became criminalized if they caused harm to the owner of the data. The condition of "harm caused" was introduced to prevent an overcriminalization of youthful computer "adventurers" who enter data banks without causing any damage. Further criminalization aims at computer sabotage and at any manipulation of other persons' data if the manipulation diminishes the usefulness of such data. The reasoning of the *Bundestag* was explicitly to protect the "high economic value" of data and to acknowledge the "increasing dependency of the economy and administrations on such data and data processing" (Deutscher Bundestag 1986, p. 34).

3. Another provision introduced "capital investment fraud" into the criminal code (para. 264a *StGB*), aiming at offenders who motivate inexperienced investors to invest in questionable projects. This provision was deemed necessary due to two recent developments: the increasing number of investment types and the growing proportion of capital invested by new social classes (e.g., professionals) with relatively

little experience in investment markets. Related provisions entered into the stock exchange act criminalized actions that suborn inexperienced persons to engage in risky option dealings (para. 89 *Börsengesetz*) and that manipulate stock rates through the spread of flawed information (para. 88 *Börsengesetz*).

4. Several other provisions were introduced. Employers who misappropriate employees' deductions to insurance and social service programs could be punished with imprisonment of up to five years or fines (para. 266 *StGB*). This is a simplification and unification of several previously existent provisions. Further, general managers or directors of banks or loan institutions who do not fulfill their obligation to announce the over-indebtedness of their institution could be punished (para. 46b and 55 *KWG*). In addition, persons who illegally lend laborers without paying social security deductions could be assigned additional punishment if their illegal behavior becomes known (para. 10 III (*AÜG*). Additional and further reaching provisions of the Social Democrats, aimed at the criminalization of illegal borrowers of labor, were defeated during the early stages of the legislative process.

While the latter provisions had been part of the original bill, one important provision was successfully introduced during the deliberations in the House. It criminalizes the forging and unauthorized use of Eurochecks, a new type of check with validity throughout Europe, and the accompanying identification cards. This was justified as necessary to protect and secure the growing system of cashless money transfer.

Two other provisions were included during the deliberations in the House at the initiative of the Social Democratic faction. One criminalized a system of "progressive sales promotion" that promises customers benefits if they gain new buyers for a particular product. The arguments for this provision were, first, that such systems entail considerable and uncalculable risks for customers inexperienced in business, and, second, potential damage to the functioning of markets. The Social Democrats also successfully introduced a provision to criminalize espionage in economic enterprises.

Other provisions included in the original bill were defeated during the House proceedings. These include a plan to penalize and fine landlords and their agents who do not appropriately communicate the rent and additional expenses to renters of housing space when a contract is made (para. 34c *GeWO*). This provision was eliminated following pressure from within the CDU/CSU. The antitrust provisions developed by the expert commission and the bid rigging provision, still part of early drafts of the Justice Department, were not part of the final bill. Attempts by Social Democrats to introduce a bid rigging provision failed in the state chamber and in the House.

In sum, the final bill passed with broad approval. While important provisions directed at firms, entrepreneurs, or top-level employees were defeated (antitrust; insufficient information of rentors), other provisions against entrepreneurial behavior did pass (fraudulent investment firms or brokers; bankrupt loan institutions) "for the sake of a functioning capital market," unanimously supported by Social Democrats and Conservatives. Several other provisions against entrepreneurial behavior passed. Yet, these were watered down in the process despite strong support from Social Democrats and after considerable opposition from the conservative faction (*Vertreterhaftung*; *Aufsichtspflichtverletzung*; fines against corporations; illegal lending of employees). Obviously, in the majority of cases under review conservatives were less ready to criminalize entrepreneurial behavior than Social Democrats. On the other hand, conservatives and Social Democrats were both ready to criminalize the behavior of lower-level employees and other lower-class people, especially in the computer sector, "to secure the functioning of the economy and of administrations," and in the area of cashless money transfer (Eurochecks), "to protect the system of cashless money transfer."

Two sets of conflict lines overlapped increasingly during the legislative process. While conflicts had originally primarily separated the legal and economic sector (e.g., committees), new interparty conflicts between conservatives representing entrepreneurial and business interests and Social Democrats representing working-class interests became increasingly relevant. Yet, where major functions of modern technologies and economic institutions are concerned and lower-class actors are the target group, both conservatives and Social Democrats are ready to criminalize. Throughout, justice criteria merge with economic criteria and power potentials of dominant classes when criminal legislation touches on economic and entrepreneurial concerns. Both economic rationales and concrete interests merge, at least under particular circumstances, to defeat the criminalization of entrepreneurial behavior even if such criminalization appears logical within the reference system of criminal law and justice.

After the Second Law: Negotiated Implementation

The Second Law Against Economic Crime was passed in 1986 after a long and frustrating process. The motivation from the early 1970s had decisively worn off. It is thus easy to tell the legislative story that followed the "Second Law." There was not any new noteworthy legislation against white-collar crime. Some of the earlier initiatives were withdrawn, for example the idea to pursue a "Third Law Against

Economic Crime" (Möhrenschlager 1984, p. 227). Further, a 1984 conference of the federal and state ministers of justice decided to terminate the systematic collection of economic crime data on the prosecutorial level. This data collection system, initiated in 1974 and coordinated by the Max Planck Institute for Foreign and International Criminal Law in Freiburg, was to be replaced by a considerably more limited system as of 1986. The Federal Justice Department was not willing to comment on who had initiated the change and if any states had voted against it (*Berckhauer and Savelsberg* 1987, p. 243).

While not much can thus be added to the legislative story, a few additional comments can be made on the implementation of criminal law against white-collar offenders. The theoretically deduced (Savelsberg 1987b) and empirically suggested (e.g., Kaiser and Meinberg 1984; Dencker and Hamm 1988) suspicion that negotiation happens in the German criminal procedure, especially in white-collar crime cases, has been confirmed in recent empirical research (Lüdemann and Bussmann 1989; Bussmann and Lüdemann 1992; Heiland and Lüdemann 1992; Schünemann 1989; Stemmler 1993). While this insight may not be surprising to the American reader, it is contradictory to the legality principle that supposedly predominates German criminal procedure and that does not leave room for negotiations. The discovery has stunned representatives of legal dogmatics and lead to interesting new dogmatic constructions (Bussmann 1991).

In short, bargaining in German courts is real and is especially pronounced in white-collar cases. Lüdemann and Bussmann's interview data with judges, prosecutors, and defense attorneys, for example, show that (partial) confessions are frequently traded against benefits such as lower penalties, the (partial) dropping of charges, limitation of evidence, and restitutive instead of penal measures. The frequency of "deals" is higher in later stages of the process and higher in economic than in general criminal cases. The difference between general and economic cases is especially pronounced in the early stages of the process—similar to Mann's (1985) American findings. Interview results indicate that this difference between general and white-collar cases is due to several factors (Lüdemann and Bussman 1989, pp. 55ff). First, justice personnel believe that the consideration of efficient procedures is especially important in white-collar cases. Second, white-collar defendants are generally assumed to be more sensitive toward punishment than other defendants, especially in the range of severe offenses. Third, defense attorneys feel more powerful in white-collar cases, partly as a result of the greater complexity of their cases, which allows for more bargaining potential. Fourth, a relatively large proportion of lawyers who work in the white-collar area believe that "deals" are legal (85% of white-collar defense attorneys). Finally, white-collar defense attorneys believe much more strongly that negotiations benefit their clients.

In sum, communicative processes and differential power potentials that were influential in the legislative process also seem to work in the legal process. What works to benefit powerful groups in legislation is also likely to provide advantages in the criminal courts.

Chapter 6
Context Structures, Situations, and Argument Structures: The Total Set of Cognitive Maps

We have, in the course of our research, analyzed a diversity of maps from the expert commission, the judicial committee, and the *Bundestag* hearing. We demonstrated in Chapter 4, in the context of the expert commission, that it is fruitful to compare different maps that emerge from various actors, situations, or structural contexts.

We now proceed to analyze a data file representing the total sample of 94 analyzed maps. We described each map through quantitative indicators for several independent variables concerning its producer, the structural context in which it emerged, the situation of presentation, and several dependent variables describing a map's formal and substantive qualities.

At the outset, two methodological caveats are needed. First, our sample is relatively small and allows for bivariate analyses at best. Second, we do not know the size and distribution of the total population of argumentative structures, although we know that the number of argumentations in a legislative process is very large. We also know that many arguments are only made orally and never documented. Other arguments may be documented but not accessible. In the context of a complex decision-making process in which a diversity of actors are involved, it is not possible to know the total population of argumentations. For these reasons we are not able to draw a representative sample.

In our selection of argumentations we referred to the following criteria. We first included all maps on the criminalization of antitrust offenses. Second, from the minutes of the expert commission we analyzed all argumentations that (a) concerned provisions later debated in the context of the Second Law Against Economic Offenses and (b) were presented by commissioners (as opposed to invited experts). Third, pragmatic criteria had to be applied. Some minutes from parliamentary committees became available only late and could not be analyzed. We also excluded all argumentations of more than 100 pages in length (with the exception of T's statement on antitrust offenses) since the analysis of one such map requires several weeks.

Independent variables measured include:

A. *Situational variables*: stage of the political process; preparedness of statement; publicity of the situation; number of participants in the situation.

B. *Actor variables*: actor code; societal sector of actor; discipline (if scholar); sector of the economy (if business); sector of law (if nonbusiness lawyer); sector of political system (if politician); political party affiliation of actor; majority/minority position in political process; type of control agency (if control agent); level of system (federal/state/local); educational background of actor.

C. *Offense variables*: offense type; degree of conflict surrounding proposition; level of public debate; type of law in which proposition is to be introduced (criminal code or *Nebenstrafrecht*); availability of non-criminal control agencies.

Table 10 gives a descriptive overview of the types of maps included in our sample for a selection of these variables. About half the maps are derived from the phase of the *Bundestag* deliberations, that is, a phase of relatively high politicization. About the same proportion of maps are based on statements by political decision makers, while one-fifth each are drawn from academics and control agents. One-quarter of the maps were analyzed from minutes of situational (oral) statements, whereas three-quarters are based on prepared (pre-written) texts. Finally, more than one-third of the analyzed statements dealt with antitrust issues, and more than one quarter with issues of corporate criminal liability.

The *dependent variables* describe the maps' formal and substantive qualities. They measure the frequency with which particular types of concepts or arguments were presented. Five groups of dependent variables can be distinguished: (a) criminal policy purposes (philosophies of punishment); (b) direction of demand (punitive/nonpunitive); (c) implementation orientation; (d) formal and (e) substantive rationalities of the argumentation. Given the diversity of themes discussed in these maps and the brief character of some of them, variables from groups (a) to (c) are characterized by many missing values. In these cases we only give a brief overview of the emerging distributions.

(a) General deterrence was the philosophy of punishment that clearly dominated these argumentative maps on economic crime. Ideas

TABLE 10. Types of Cognitive Maps Analyzed

Variables	Values	Percent of maps
Phase	1972 Meeting of Lawyers Association	19.1
	Expert commission	9.6
	Ministries	14.9
	State Chamber (*Bundesrat*)	5.3
	House of Representatives (*Bundestag*)	51.1
Degree of preparedness	Ad hoc statements	25.5
	Prepared statements	35.1
	Papers presented	8.5
	Expert opinions	8.5
	Explanation of bill	22.3
Sector of actor	Academia	19.1
	Economy	7.4
	Criminal justice	13.8
	Other control agencies	4.2
	Polity	52.1
Propositions maps relate to	Antitrust offenses	36.2
	Improper lending of employees	14.9
	Computer offenses	10.6
	Liability of/within organizations	26.6
	Capital investment offenses	7.4
	Stock exchange offenses	3.2

of retribution and incapacitation were never mentioned, rehabilitation was mentioned in one map, and restitution in six of the 94 maps. This tendency fits widespread beliefs in the rational character of economic crime that can be most easily fought by increasing the expected costs of being detected and punished.

(b) This strong general deterrence orientation was also reflected in the direction of demands. Forty-five maps aimed at the creation of new criminal provisions, five at the toughening of existing ones. The abolition of provisions is not discussed in any map. Twenty-three argumentations considered the specification, and ten the full implementation of existing norms. The strengthening of control agencies was discussed in twelve of the cases. Nonpunitive strategies were clearly in the minority. Eleven maps dealt with private law, and fourteen with administrative law provisions. Obviously, the early framing of the debate by the criminal law section of the Justice Department was reflected in the overall focus of the debates.

(c) Ever since the early 1970s the recognition has grown that simply

TABLE 11. Complexity of Maps by Preparedness

Complexity	Preparedness			Total
	Ad hoc statement	Prepared statement	Paper/expert opinion explanation of bill	
Low	19	15	13	47
High	5	18	24	47
Total	24	33	37	94

Chi square = 11.70966; df = 2; p = 0.0029

passing laws may have little effect on social reality if the implementation structures are not taken into consideration (e.g., Mayntz 1980, 1982; Wollmann 1980). We were therefore interested in the number of arguments that dealt with the implementation of whatever norms had been proposed. We counted each argument that dealt with the implementation of a proposition by any of the implementing agencies in each map. We found that only a few maps take implementation strategies into consideration. No map referred to police work, the courts, or correctional institutions. Four maps referred to prosecuting agencies, three to other control agencies. The small number of arguments that are concerned with the implementation of provisions supports Schubarth's (1980) thesis that criminal law making is dominated by legal dogmatic reasoning with relatively little representation of legal realism. While some economic arguments were counted and while belief in general deterrence dominated the debate, little attention was given to the implementation of the proposed provisions by the agencies of criminal justice.

(d) We measured the degree of purposive rationality for each of the 94 maps to identify the conditions under which such rationality can be achieved. Since decision making in a complex environment requires the consideration of a large number of factors, we measured the number of concepts considered by different speakers as a necessary condition for purposive rationality. In the analysis we dichotomized simple maps (up to six concepts) and complex maps (more than six concepts).[1]

Not surprisingly, there is a clear correlation between the complexity of a map and the degree of preparedness (see Table 11). We also found that the complexity of maps increases with the closeness to binding decisions (chi square = 23.86; df = 2; p < .0005). While simple maps predominate during the early phases of the Lawyers Association meetings and even during the work of the expert commission (despite a few

1. We present only contingency tables with statistically significant results.

TABLE 12. Complexity of Maps by Government Branch

Complexity	Government branch		Total
	Parliament	Administration	
Low	20	6	26
High	1	19	20
Total	21	25	46

Chi square = 20.75912; df = 1; p = 0.0000

very complex maps), maps in the legislative process tend to be complex. This correlation also holds when we control for the preparedness of the argumentation. These results are only statistically significant for the category "written expert opinions and prepared lectures" (chi square = 24.05; df = 1; p < .0005).

Within the political sector, in the final phase of the decision-making process, argumentations of ministerial bureaucrats are much more complex than those of parliamentarians (see Table 12). We continue to measure this relation when we control for the preparedness of the statements. The correlation between political sector and complexity continues to be significant within the categories "ad hoc statements" and "written expert opinions and prepared lectures." These correlations can be easily explained. First, ministerial bureaucracies have much more specialized expertise at their disposal than do parliamentarians. This is particularly true in the German political system where parliamentarians have much smaller staffs than their colleagues in the U.S. Congress. Second, ministerial bureaucrats argue much more frequently not just for or against a proposition but, along more differentiated lines, about particular formulations.

We further tested a hypothesis on the relation between minority/majority status and complexity of argumentation. Gallhofer and Saris (1984), for example, find that in foreign policy decision making the pressure to argue extensively is greater on those with minority opinions than among those who are assured of a majority. The relation is not confirmed in our analysis. Forty argumentative maps could be classified as majority or minority positions (in terms of parliamentary strength of political parties). While only about half of the majority argumentations were simple (51.7%), the same is true for 72.7 percent of the minority maps (see Table 13). This difference can be partly explained by the fact that sixteen of the majority maps are lectures, expert statements, or legislative explanations to the bill (see Table 14). Again, we controlled for preparedness of the argumentations. If we

TABLE 13. Complexity of Maps by Majority/Minority

Complexity	Majority	Minority	Total
Low	15	8	23
High	14	3	17
Total	29	11	40

Chi square = 1.43; df = 1; p = 0.2302. Due to the low number of cases the chi square test cannot be interpreted.

TABLE 14. Complexity of Maps by Majority/Minority for Relatively Prepared Statements

Complexity	Majority	Minority	Total
Low	2	3	5
High	14	2	16
Total	16	5	21

Chi square = 4.73814; df = 1; p = 0.0295. Due to the low number of cases the chi square test cannot be interpreted.

only consider ad hoc statements all thirteen majority maps are simple. Only one of the six minority ad hoc statements was complex. These findings thus suggest that (a) the Saris/Gallhofer hypothesis is contradicted if we include argumentations from the ministerial bureaucracy into our sample; and (b) it is not confirmed even if we limit the analysis to relatively unprepared statements of parliamentarians (see Tables 13 and 14).

Another way to distinguish majority and minority positions is along sector lines, that is, between criminal lawyers (majority) and private lawyers (plus one economist; minority). All maps of the private law/ economists' minority are complex in nature, while two-thirds of the criminal lawyers' maps are simple (chi square = 7.2; df = 1; p < .05). Here a hypothesis derived from decision theory finds support according to which minority contributors to a debate feel stronger pressure toward complex explanation. We had demonstrated above that economic lawyers were not only a minority in disciplinary terms, but also in political terms as proponents of a less penal strategy to solve the economic crime problem. This latter relation, however, is statistically uncertain since it is based on only eighteen cases (see Table 15).

(e) Finally, we analyzed substantive rationalities of our maps. We were first interested in arguments with punitive versus antipunitive implications. We counted those arguments as punitive that either stress negative impacts of crime or positive impacts of penal responses. Anti-

TABLE 15. Complexity of Maps by Majority/Minority
for Relatively Unprepared Statements

Complexity	Majority	Minority	Total
Low	9	1	10
High	4	4	8
Very high	0	1	1
Total	13	6	19

Chi square = 5.57820; df = 2; p = 0.0615. Due to the low
number of cases the chi square test cannot be interpreted.

punitive are those arguments that point to negative consequences of criminal punishment or discuss the societal conditions of offenses and thus suggest strategies against these underlying structural factors. We dichotomized these variables and distinguished between maps that contained none versus one or more of the punitive or antipunitive arguments. We counted the number of each of these types of arguments, and we created additional indices by summarizing all punitive and antipunitive variables. Finally, we created one additional index by subtracting all negative (nonpunitive) from all positive (punitive) arguments in each map. The resulting values were recoded and resulted in a scale from -2 (anti-punitive) to $+2$ (punitive). We then conducted bivariate contingency analyses, measuring the relation between different structural and situational (independent) variables and the punitive content of argumentations (dependent variable).

We were first interested in the relation between party membership and punitiveness. Relations between party and presentation of negative impacts of penal measures were not statistically significant (chi square = 3.3; df = 2; p < .1). Yet, Social Democrats were more likely to point to positive consequences of punitive measures than conservatives (see Table 16). We also find a relation between party membership and the comprehensive index of punitiveness (thus taking all four types of arguments into consideration). The relation identified for a few maps of the judicial committee (Chapter 5), also holds for the total set of cognitive maps. In debates on economic crime issues, Social Democrats tend to be more punitive than conservatives, (chi square = 26.65; df = 6; p < .01). Larger sets of cognitive maps are necessary to provide for statistically more rigid testing.

Furthermore, maps with a predominance of punitive arguments are more likely to be presented in the early stages of the process, that is, during the Lawyers Association meetings and the expert commission's

TABLE 16. Maps Expressing Positive Impacts of Criminalizations by Political Party and Administration

Mentioning of positive impacts of criminalization	SPD	CDU/CSU	Administration	Total
None	5	10	6	21
Some	1	2	3	6
Many	3	0	8	11
Total	9	12	17	38

Chi square = 8.56540; df = 4; p = 0.0729. Due to the low number of cases the chi square test cannot be interpreted.

work than in the legislative process (chi square = 13.89; df = 4; p < .01). Within the legislative process we find more arguments that hint at the negative impacts of punitive measures in the later parliamentary phase than in the ministerial phase. This corresponds with the finding that relatively few pro-punitive arguments were presented in the preparation phase and that, during the legislative process, punitive arguments are more dominant in the ministerial than in the parliamentary phase (chi square = 19.05; df = 8; p < .05). Yet, the relation between phase of the political process and punitiveness was not significant when we used the punitiveness scale (chi square = 21.02; df = 16; p < .5). The correlation between phase and punitiveness is obviously watered down when we take the more ambivalent indicators for punitiveness into account (conditions of offense; negative impacts of offense).

The correlation between phase and the stronger indicator for punitiveness (positive versus negative impacts of criminal punishment) confirms our earlier finding that scholarly experts make less ambiguous statements on the value of punitive measures in the parliamentary hearing than in the early commission phase (Chapter 4).

We summarize some additional results below. Punitive arguments are more likely in less prepared statements (chi square = 21; df = 8; p < .01) and in contexts with fewer participants (chi square = 10.08; df = 4; p < .05). This is supported by earlier observations according to which some experts were clearly punitive in early ad hoc statements (e.g., during the Lawyers Association meetings), but much more differentiated in more extensive expert opinions they presented during the commission's work. Further, positions of the opposition party are, in this law-making process, much more likely to be punitive than those of the majority party (chi square = 10.04; df = 3; p < .05). In our case this simply means that the Social Democrats, on the opposition bench for most of the period under investigation, were more punitive in a legislative process against economic crime than the conservatives. This confirms earlier theoretical assumptions and empirical indications.

In sum, the analysis of the total set of cognitive maps further confirms several hypotheses for which earlier chapters had provided qualitative support. Future research should provide larger samples allowing for multivariate analyses of the hypotheses tested here.

Part IV
Conclusions from the Case Study and an American-German Comparison

Chapter 7
Rationalities, Communication, and Power: Conclusions

We have studied the political process through which economic behavior is criminalized and defended against criminalization. We have investigated all relevant phases of this process for the Second Law Against Economic Crime. They include the early claims making by media, the legal profession, and public opinion; the work of the expert commission; and the legislative process, in different departments of the administration, and in the two chambers of parliament (*Bundestag*). One of our central theoretical concerns was the question of how different theories within legal sociology relate to the empirical reality of criminal legislation against economic offenses in West Germany. We selected theoretical approaches according to the dimensions of functionalism versus action/conflict-group theory and Marxist versus differentiation or pluralism theory. According to Alber (1982) differentiation and conflict-group theories are best suited to explain the development of welfare law. Do they also explain criminal law making as a "negative" complement to "positive" welfare state policies?

Our empirical data yielded several answers to this question. Again, a case study does not allow verification or clear falsification of rather complex theories. It can suggest, however, modifications of their hypotheses and help to develop further research questions. First, according to Sack's (1983) prescriptive model of criminal policy we should not expect criminalizing reactions to new types of deviant behavior in welfare states. Rather, adequate reactions would be adaptations of the normative system or policies that try to change those social structures that have caused deviance. In Germany, the reactions to new types of economic deviance certainly do not follow Sack's prescriptions. Instead there is a clear trend toward criminalization through the creation of new criminal provisions and the reorganization of segments of the criminal justice system.

In the case of the Second Law Against Economic Crime, this predominantly punitive reaction was modified and softened, especially as the process progressed. This may have been due to the inclusion of economic law specialists in the commission that prepared the package of measures against economic crime. It is an open question, though, whether the economic law orientation was based on the welfare state orientation of experts and decision makers. It may well have been supported by purely economic rationales, or, as our data on price fixing suggest, by the interests of party clienteles, concerned powerful classes, or by the functional needs of economic sectors as perceived by decision makers.

The proponents of (neo-) Marxist functionalist approaches (e.g., Pilgram and Steinert 1975; Steinert 1978) try to explain the development of criminal law in terms of functional needs of the capitalist economy, modes of production, or abstract interests of important sectors or units within the economy. Our case provided us with impressive illustrations of such theses, including the criminalization of computer offenses, misuse of credit cards, and capital investment fraud.

The functionalist aspect of this theory type, however, is problematic. Also in this legislative process, state and economy turn out to be highly differentiated. First, there are a wide variety of concerns or functions, in class-specific as well as in sector-specific terms, that are affected by the laws under investigation. Second, we found conflict processes, lines, and coalitions within each sector to be highly differentiated and shifting as the debate moved from one proposition to the next. Third, the representatives of different state control agencies (e.g., trust control administration and prosecutors) with various organization-specific interests were highly represented in the law-making process. Their interests are certainly not in accordance with those of industry and frequently not in harmony with each other. Instead, each group attempts to extend its resources and control capacities. Fourth, concrete and articulated interests of economic actors may well be in conflict with long-term functional needs of the economy and yet nonetheless prevail, as shown in the price fixing and (especially) the bid rigging cases. Finally, political actors may directly follow a political rationale that aims at an extension of their individual or party power resources. Votes are an important resource in democratic systems, and politicians must not neglect the interests of their constituency. The result of law-making processes thus depends, in the parliamentary phase, largely on the representation of different classes or strata in parliament. The functionalist aspect of Marxist-functionalist theory may therefore appear plausible in the case of some provisions, but it is seriously questioned in the view of others.

The arguments against the functionalist approach support the action/conflict-group orientation in Turkel's (1980) analysis. His Marxist-guided theses also find partial support. Turkel assumes an increasing intrusion of powerful economic actors' substantive rationalities upon formal legal discourse. This prediction is particularly supported by the arguments of CDU/CSU representatives and industry's successful fight against the criminalization of price fixing.

Yet our analysis also raises considerable doubts about the Marxist approach. First, unions and consumer organizations were also represented in the law-making process. Second, criminal legislation and the reorganization of control agencies had at least some success against economic offenders, some of whom are of higher status and more powerful than the average offender. Third, Turkel's discussion of "powerful economic actors" does not sufficiently reflect the diversity of concerns involved in our case study. Fourth, his approach cannot explain the successful autonomous (i.e., organization-specific) interests of agents of formalized social control that played a major role in this law-making process.

If the Marxist approach should be of explanatory value for our case, its terms have to be specified. What proportion of the success of "powerful economic actors" can be explained by class-specific interests and what proportion by sector-specific interests? The attempt to criminalize price fixing was rejected first by entrepreneurs (a class-specific argument) and then by an intra-sector coalition of unions and industry federations (a sector-specific argument). The question which argument has more explanatory power can only be answered by further comparative analysis.

Haferkamp (1980, 1984) follows an action theory approach. He specifies the conflict-group perspective by understanding criminal justice policy as domination group-related policy. He assumes that the increasing functional differentiation of modern societies results in a loss of domination. As a consequence, he expects increasing decriminalization or the redistribution of chances to become criminalized from lower to higher classes or domination groups.

Haferkamp's action theory approach is certainly confirmed by our study, unlike the functionalist principle. This aspect of his perspective is consistent with our findings on the activism of industry associations in their prevention of the price fixing provisions. Our data also support Haferkamp's domination theory perspective, especially the argumentations of the political representatives. When they deal with an atypical group of offenders (in terms of domination, i.e., entrepreneurs) they exchange typical arguments: conservatives used abolitionist and Social Democrats used criminalizing arguments. Yet our study also shows that, in the pre-parliamentarian stages of decision making, conflict lines were more sector-specific than domination-group related. We conclude that the domination-group perspective becomes more relevant as criminal law making moves closer to the public stage of politics. Haferkamp's decriminalization hypothesis is contradicted by our case. Law makers react to growing or new forms of economic offenses primarily with criminal justice programs. The initiatives for criminalization are mainly, although not exclusively, taken by Social Democrats. As representatives of the more dominated classes they should, according to Sack's theory of criminal law in the welfare state, be expected to be the forerunners of decriminalization. Yet this new criminalizing tendency of the Social Democrats could be explained, with Haferkamp, as an attempt to redistribute chances to become criminalized from dominated to dominant classes. The Social Democratic initiatives and the industry and Christian Democratic defenses were never as intense and insistent as when entrepreneurs were concerned in the price-fixing case.

Yet, while our case study documents attempts to redistribute criminal punishment from the lower to the upper classes, the arguments of criminalizers are based on stereotypical and partially false images of economic offenders as high-status offenders (Berckhauer 1980). The redistribution hypothesis is thus not valid for a considerable part of economy-related criminalizations. Even if these criminal law programs are initiated with a redistributive intention, and even if they are well suited for symbolic policies, their impacts are unpredictable and possible counterproductive. This may hold even more when the selective implementation of successfully generated criminal laws is also considered (for Canada, see Hagan and Parker 1985; for the US, Mann, Wheeler, and Sarat 1980; Wheeler and Rothman 1982; Wheeler, Weisburd, and Bode 1982; for Germany, Savelsberg 1988; Bussmann 1991; Bussmann and Lüdemann 1992; Heiland and Lüdemann 1992).

Weber's central predictions are supported by our case. First, the creation and expansion of a specific economy-related criminal law, including specialized control agencies, support his particularization hypothesis. We also found evidence for Weber's prediction of an increasing intrusion of substantive rationalities as an impact of particularization. Weber's observations and our findings lead to a more general hypothesis: *Increasing legalization and a parallel differentiation of the legal system increase problems of integration within the legal system itself.* As a consequence we expect an opening of particular fields of law and their implementing agencies to rationalities of those social spheres or units they are supposed to control.

In short, our case supports an action theoretical approach to criminal law making and challenges functionalism. On an other dimension it suggests an integration of neo-Marxist and differentiation-theoretical or pluralist arguments. The outcome of the law-making process can thus be understood as a result of interest-oriented social action that mobilizes power and utilizes institutionalized channels of communication. More conclusions can be drawn with regard to these concepts.

Interests and Rationalities

In the case of bid rigging, manifest interests have proven more effective than perceived long-term systemic interests or functional demands of the economy. In general, manifest economic interests were forcefully and successfully articulated in the legislative process we investigated. Bustos et al. (1982) come to similar conclusions for environmental legislation in Spain. These findings challenge generalized theses that societal groups lack specific interests with regard to criminal law (e.g., Waldmann 1979).

Hagan (1980) also finds a clear engagement of interest groups in his comparative analysis of 43 case studies on criminal legislation in the United States. Manifest interests of business and capital, however, play but a subordinate role in these cases. Our case shows that these results cannot be generalized. They must be explained through the specific types of crime under investigation in these 43 studies: juvenile delinquency, alcohol and drug-related offenses, and prostitution. Interest groups that are frequently pointed out in these studies have earlier been recognized as central by Becker (1973), the implementors of criminal law, and related professional groups (see recently Kassebaum and Ward 1991).

In the legislative work on the Second Law Against Economic Crime, we find interests of professional groups, agencies of social control, and welfare bureaucracies represented, as well as interests of powerful industry organizations. The degree of participation and type of position of a diversity of interest groups varied with the particular offenses under consideration. Representatives of industry argued in favor of criminalization, for example, in the case of computer crime; in other cases they were strictly opposed to the creation of new criminal provisions, for example, in the case of bid rigging. Among the agencies of social control, prosecutors mostly pleaded for new criminalization and for the removal of procedural safeguards. This hardly comes as a surprise because such initiatives would result in an increase in organizational competence and jurisdiction, a facilitation of the charging process, improved career chances, and improved legitimation of prosecution against white-collar offenses.

The interests of trust control agencies proved to be ambivalent. The criminalization of antitrust offenses would have resulted in a higher legitimacy and weight of antitrust intervention; yet, competencies and jurisdictions would have been redirected from antitrust agencies to prosecutorial agencies. This ambivalence was expressed in changing positions of the federal antitrust agency (*Bundeskartellamt*).

Conflict and Consensus

Given the diversity of partly contradictory interests, we expect debates and decision processes in which these interests are articulated to be conflictual. We follow Dahrendorf's (1974) plea for a specific and differentiated use of "conflict," applying the term only to the action theoretical level (as manifest conflict).[1]

The concept of conflict in the tradition of Hobbes and Mills was, especially during the 1960s and 1970s, introduced into the sociology of criminal justice against a long predominant consensus model. Originally criminal law was perceived as the core of a crystallized and sedimented normative societal consensus of society (Durkheim 1893). This understanding has been successfully rejected by recent empirical and theoretical studies. Hopkins (1975), however, has criticized the absoluteness of the conflict/consensus debate. He points to the varying size of potential conflict groups, which sometimes include the overwhelming majority of the general population. In the latter case conflict might be transformed to consensus. In another criticism, criminal law norms may have been generated in conflictual processes but become consensual through their institutionalization. In his investigation of the Austrian criminal code reform, Pohoryles (1981) demonstrates that even in those cases where diverse positions and diverging tendencies existed in public debates, political decision making often was *not* characterized by open conflict. In addition, with the exception of quite specific cases such as abortion, decision makers preferred nonconflictual decision making.

A strongly consensual tendency is apparent in our study of the Second Law Against Economic Crime as well. Two different administrations presented an identical legislative proposal to parliament. The first administration was dominated by the Social Democratic Party, the second by the conservative Christian Democrats, while both administrations included the same junior coalition partner, the Free Demo-

---

1. We distinguish on preceding theoretical levels between objective structural conditions (contradictions) and the definition of these conditions by actors. Conflictual processes may result from those conditions and definitions.

crats. But even after the change of government in 1982, the government bill and the alternative bill of the Social Democratic faction were identical for most provisions. Finally, the bill was passed with the votes of the majority factions of Christian Democrats and Free Democrats and the minority faction of the Social Democrats.

Yet we have already seen that the process was also characterized by diverse opinions and openly conflictual processes, especially in the case of antitrust offenses. The principal argument of Waldmann (1979) against a conflict-theoretical model for the understanding of criminal law making is thus challenged, especially when he points to the lack of identifiable conflict groups, perceivable confrontations, or interests of target groups. This part of our observations instead supports demands by Quinney (1975) that an interest and conflict theoretical approach must be taken seriously within the sociology of criminal law, that we must understand criminal law as the outcome of conflictual processes, in which interests of specific societal groups are reflected.

Our analysis of the conflictual processes and debates on different provisions of the Second Law Against Economic Crime demonstrates the diversity and complexity of these fields of conflict. Conflict lines are drawn through the parliamentary and administrative systems. They shift in the course of the legislative process. They separate diverse groups for different provisions of the same bill. In one case or stage they separate representatives of different societal systems (e.g., economy versus law); in the other they separate representatives of different political parties.

At any rate, conflicting interests are not automatically reflected in the legislative process. They often need to be communicated and backed by power.

Communication and Power

We demonstrated the importance of communication and its strongly institutionalized character when we discussed the communication between the political sector and economic lobbying organizations. In sum, 179 communications were registered in the BDI archives between October 1975 and January 1981. The number of nonregistered communications is unknown but probably larger. Most communications are concentrated in four rather limited time periods in which the most important decisions of the political sector were expected. The largest part (66%) of these communications served the coordination and collection of arguments within the economic sector. The most interested organizations of the economic sector considered a joint and coordinated procedure as crucial to successful prevention of criminal legislation against antitrust offenses. Most communications by economic organizations to the political sector were directed at ministries, only a small portion at the parliament. Whereas the exchange of early phases was mostly between associations of the economy, exchanges in later phases were mostly between associations and ministries. The more final political decisions became, the higher was the hierarchical level on which information was exchanged, in ministries as well as in the Federation of German Industry.

During each step in this communication process the intention to penalize antitrust offenses was further reduced. First, jurisprudents of trade law in the expert commission had diminished the intentions of jurisprudents of criminal law to criminalize a diversity of behaviors. Yet they joined the criminal jurisprudents in their intention to penalize particularly severe antitrust offenses. Second, from among these provisions only one aiming at the criminalization of bid rigging reached the bill of the Department of Justice. Third, even this proposition was not included in the government bill finally passed on to the *Bundestag*.

The analysis of the activities of industry associations, especially of *one* department of *one* federal association on *one* individual proposition and the communications exchanged in this process, demonstrated the high complexity and institutionalization of communicative processes between the economy and the political sector. It challenges assumptons of a quasi-automatic adaptation of decisions to interests of the economy. Highly publicized donation or corruption affairs are only a small supplement to this institutionalized apparatus of lobbying which consistently and in organizationally secured routine addresses the political sector. This apparatus is directed at three factors: forming concerns and knowledge structures of political actors; supplying sympathizers within the political system with arguments; and stressing threatening impacts of planned political decisions in the perceptions of decision makers (especially impacts resulting from decisions in the economic sector: the closing of firms, the removal of investment, the layoff of workers). Such power potentials support the effectiveness of a highly complex and routinized communication process.

One final remark on the German case study: The routinized communication process we have described becomes mobilized in the late phases of the political process. The result of this process thus differs considerably from the intentions of those moral entrepreneurs who initiated it. The moral entrepreneurs remind us of the sorcerer's apprentice described in Goethe's famous poem, who managed to make the waters run but was almost washed away by them with all he possessed.

Chapter 8
The American and German Cases: Commonalities and Differences

We have followed the recent German history of white-collar crime legislation through several phases, including claims making, expert consulting, drafting, and legislation. We found some theoretical propositions confirmed, others challenged (see Chapter 7). For example, the initial intent of claims makers to redistribute the chances of criminal punishment by increasing the likelihood of upper-class offenders to be arrested, prosecuted, and sentenced did not materialize. Social forces that were active in the claims-making process differed from those that were influential in the political process. On a more abstract level, we found that legislative innovation of criminal statutes may serve functional needs of the economic sector, but does so only under particular cirumstances. This finding underlined the need to pursue an action or conflict group oriented analysis.

Our findings are, of course, embedded in a country-specific context. How generalizable are they in international comparison? We attempt to give a limited response by providing a comparative account of movements, law enforcement activities, and legislation against white-collar offenses in the United States.[1] We present American findings concerning phases and actors comparable to those investigated in our German case study. We consider claims making and the legislative and

---

1. Ideally, we would analyze a large sample of cases from a many countries. Yet the number of potential cases is limited. Furthermore, each case is so complex that such data gathering would be an extremely costly endeavor. It is thus not possible to establish a large sample of cases to test systematically a set of hypotheses. The study of complex processes is thus limited to providing empirical evidence on one case or a small set of cases. As we have argued above, this procedure can help in the development of theory. Case study evidence suggests modifications of overly streamlined theories. International comparison can point to nation-specific limits and cross-national generalizations of theories.

administrative responses. We find cross-national similarities and differences and suggest preliminary explanations for both.

Claims Making and Social Movement in the United States: Public, Moral Entrepreneurs, and Centralized Response

Critical sentiments against white-collar offenders are nothing new in the United States. In particular situations these sentiments have been stirred up and have then led to social movements against the holders of positions of power. Examples are concerns expressed around the turn of the century, during the 1930s, and again (and most insistently) since the late 1960s. We sketch the historical background of the debate and then look, first at the most recent movement against white-collar offenders, and second at the centralized responses to the issue.

Transgressions of the Powerful: A Long Debate in America

Claims making against white-collar crime is older in America than in Germany. Edwin Sutherland's scholarly attack, launched first in his 1939 Presidential Address to the American Sociological Association, is well known (Sutherland 1940; also 1945). Sutherland developed his arguments into a book in which he argued that

persons of the upper socio-economic class engage in much criminal behavior; . . . this behavior differs from the criminal behavior of the lower socioeconomic class principally in the administrative procedures which are used in dealing with the offenders. (Sutherland 1949, p. 9)

Sutherland does not find any difference in the etiology of criminal behavior between social classes, but strong differences with regard to government responses. His attack on white-collar crime was preceded by less well known earlier concerns. At the beginning of this century Edward Ross (1907) expressed his worries about the dependency of Americans on complex institutions over which they had no control. This dependency, Ross argued, resulted in a vulnerability that would easily be exploited. It would be exploited by a "criminaloid" class whose actions, while not defined criminal by the law, were comparable to most common crimes (Shrager and Short 1980, pp. 14–15). When Ross wrote, the federal government had already taken first action. In 1890, for example, Congress passed the "Sherman Antitrust Act" to protect consumers against antitrust offenses. But such responses were neither typical nor backed by remarkable enforcement power.

More vigorous government action against white-collar (and especially corporate) crime emerged during the 1930s, through legislation and law enforcement (Sutherland 1949, p. 27). Sutherland suggests that this vigor reflected the loss of trust in business after the 1929 crash of the stock exchange and the subsequent Great Depression. The New Deal era was, as is well known, characterized by a basic shift in philosophy and policy with regard to the control of business. The Roosevelt administration created numerous regulatory agencies during this period including the Securities and Exchange Commission and the National Labor Relations Board.

The decades following the 1930s witnessed less concern for crimes of the powerful. Only one singular event of highly visible law enforcement against powerful white-collar offenders occured, the 1961 antitrust case against several major producers of heavy electrical equipment (Geis 1992). This neglect was paralleled in criminological research which largely distanced itself from the study of white-collar crime. Geis argues that the disregard of crimes of the powerful in scholarship and in enforcement during this period may be

an aftermath of earlier times, when challenges to establish centers of power could prove hazardous, especially during the reign of Senator Joseph McCarthy. The cold war standoff between the United States and the Soviet Union also had produced an uneasy acceptance of the status quo." (Geis 1985, p. 67)

Yet the period of disregard of the transgressions and crimes of the powerful would come to an end in the late 1960s.

The New Movement Against White-Collar Crime

The historical experience seems to suggest that crimes of the powerful are more likely to be attacked, by law enforcement agencies and intellectuals alike, in an open society, in a nonrepressive climate, and, possibly closely connected, in times when societies do not experience any major and immediate threat from the outside. In addition, Sutherland argues that government action against corporations and high-status actors is most likely in times of mistrust against public institutions, especially institutions of economic power. Such times returned during the second half of the 1960s and the early 1970s. The reasons for mistrust differed only partially from those of the 1930s. They include a long series of troubling events and bad political news, including the Vietnam War, protest movements and urban violence, the discovery of corruption in high places, and Watergate, finally supplemented by bad economic news following the 1973 oil embargo (Lipset and Schneider 1983).

Times of Public Mistrust

Concerns with transgressions by the powerful certainly emerged in the general public and publicized opinion. Cullen et al. (1987, p. 151), in their analysis of the successful prosecution against Ford Motor Corporation in the Ford Pinto case, compile several indicators for the growing public mistrust against corporate America, for example:

—In 1965, an average of 68 percent of citizens polled on their attitudes toward eight major industries stated that they had "very" or "mostly" favorable feelings. By 1977 that figure had dropped to 35.5 percent . . .
—Asked how much "confidence" they had in the "people running major companies," less than one-third of a national sample contacted in 1973 and 1974 answered "a great deal." By the early 1980s, this had slipped even further to 26 percent. (Cullen et al. 1987, p. 151)

As we showed in Chapter 3, public trust in entrepreneurs also slipped in Germany during the same period. Here we observe an amazing parallel between the two countries, suggesting that other than purely national forces were at work. This shift in public opinion was accompanied, again in both countries, by a movement to challenge the actions of the powerful and to demand that misdeeds be controlled by government and punished by agencies of criminal justice.

In Germany, claims making against powerful economic offenders increased rapidly in selected German news media during the 1970s (Chapter 3). The legal profession also got involved in the claims-making process. We demonstrated in our discussion of the 1972 Meeting of the German Lawyers Association that this move was motivated partly by moral entrepreneurs in the Association's own ranks. It was accompanied by prosecutorial initiatives and organizational reforms of state criminal justice agencies. Finally, all these initiatives were followed by the initiation of the federal commission for the fight against economic crime (Chapter 4) and by the legislative process (Chapters 5 and 6).

In the United States as well, the increasing public mistrust against powerful institutions and their agents turned into a movement to control and punish harmful actions of powerful offenders—the second parallel between events in the two countries. Yet the American movement seems to have taken somewhat different forms. There is no systematic analysis of the changing patterns of economic crime reporting in American news media in the beginning states of the claims-making process, even though exemplary evidence provided by Cullen et al. (1987, p. 1) indicates that newspapers and magazines did pay considerable attention to this issue, at least by the early 1980s. The core and the initiation of the movement, however, appear to have been located with other social forces.

The Role of Prosecutors

One important carrier of the emergent movement during the 1970s were prosecutors. Katz (1980) argues that prosecutors actually drove the movement against offenders among professionals and powerful actors in government and corporations. While encouraged by the breaking of several scandals, the prosecutors' initiative was also promoted by newly emerging capacities of the prosecutors' offices and by new career opportunities:

. . . the movement in the last decade [1970s] was propelled as a nationally led, right-wing influence on local offices suddenly dissolved with Watergate. Preexisting trends were allowed free expression. The trends included a general if gentle meritocratic movement; the rapid expansion of social welfare programs in the 1960s without carefully planned controls; pressure from Naderism for action against consumer fraud; and the cycle of the "Go-Go 60s" and the recession of the early 1970s, which threw many businesses into bancruptcy when the crimes of the past were suddenly matters of public record. . . . "Watergate" marked the end of repression against war and race protestors and destroyed the "street crime" campaign of the Nixon Administration, removing law enforcement concerns that had obfuscated trends toward increased attention on white-collar crime. . . . At the same time, Watergate provided historically unprecedented opportunities for professional mobility to a national set of aggressive lawyers. (Katz 1980, p. 175)

The prosecutorial movement against powerful offenders appears to have been a decentralized initiative. It was not the result of conscious policy shifts of the federal administration. Instead, the impetus came (a) from the field level and (b) from a diversity of agencies. While this movement within control agencies predated Watergate and thus reflected a longer trend beginning during the 1960s, the specifically American "historical accident" of Watergate gave the decisive impetus. It legitimized those who had wanted to push the white-collar issue for some time and it created potentials for their professional mobility.

It should be noted, though, that the legal movement against white-collar offenders remained largely "symbolic," according to Katz (1980) and Cullen et al. (1987), reaffirming the legitimacy of the legal system without challenging major institutional arrangements. In addition, the majority of defendants in white-collar cases were not among the powerful—even though several sensational cases against powerful offenders were prosecuted.

Notwithstanding an occasional "big-name" defendant . . . much of the activity that U.S. attorneys label "white-collar crime prosecution" is not directed at executives but at lower-echelon personnel who do not enjoy the protection of political or economic power. (Cullen et al. 1987, p. 23)

The prosecutorial origin of the American movement against white-collar offenders, stressed by Katz, influenced the outcome of the movement in at least two ways. First, challenges of the powerful were driven by a "case motif" and did not aim at institutional reform (Katz 1980, p. 168). Second, "law making" in response to the newly perceived forms of dangerous behavior resulted, according to Katz, less from legislative initiatives than from prosecutors who instrumentalized non-white-collar laws for white-collar purposes. Prosecutors used, for example, anti-racketeering laws (e.g., RICO) against members of legitimate organizations, clearly against the legislative intent. Or they set new standards by pursuing unprecedented kinds of prosecutions.

The best illustration for the latter is the landmark case against the Ford Motor Corporation in the Ford Pinto case. In their in-depth analysis of this case, Cullen et al. (1987) confirm the importance of the prosecutorial initiative. But they extend Katz's argument to discuss the role of additional actors in this process.

Moral Entrepreneurs and Criminologists

One of the most outstanding examples among the moral entrepreneurs was the consumer advocate Ralph Nader. His 1965 book *Unsafe at any Speed* became a "penetrating and widely discussed" (Cullen et al. 1987, p. 162) bestseller, right at the outset of the time of declining public confidence. Nader asserted that the automobile industry was so concerned with profits that it grossly neglected safety issues. American industry, especially the auto sector, was seriously challenged:

Largely as a result of exposés by Ralph Nader, the auto industry has been the subject of increasing criticism for its lack of ethics, violations of law, and general disregard for the safety of consumers. (Clinard and Yeager, cited after Cullen et al. 1987, p. 154)

The effect of Nader's efforts was accelerated when it became public that agents of General Motors had spied on Nader to discredit him (Fisse and Braithwaite 1983). The affair created forceful responses, for example and most noteworthy, at the 1966 Public Hearings of the Senate Committee on the Judiciary. The scandal may even have had legislative impact:

It is not coincidental that in 1966 . . . the U.S. Congress passed the Highway Safety Act, which mandated federal regulation of the automotive industry and led to the creation of an enforcement agency, the National Highway Traffic Safety Administration. (Cullen et al. 1987, p. 155)

Scholars of crime and criminal justice also contributed to the rising awareness of crimes of the powerful and to the privileged treatment they received in the system of social control, especially in the institutions of criminal justice (Cullen et al. 1987, pp. 14–16). For example, by the mid-1980s several noteworthy collections of essays on white-collar crime had appeared (e.g., Geis and Strotland 1980; Edelhertz and Overcast 1982; Fisse and French 1985). Furthermore, a remarkable set of publications, reflecting the work of a group of scholars at Yale University, included numerous journal publications and a book series on issues ranging from white-collar defense (Mann 1985) and sentencing (Weisburd et al. 1991) to administrative control (Shapiro 1984).

Again, the American trend is part of an international pattern, as indicated by the number of white-collar related criminological publications in an international bibliography (Liebl and Liebl 1985). The average annual number of publications listed (mostly concentrated on American and German literature) for the first half of this century is dismal: around two publications per year during the first two decades and between five and ten publications per year between 1920 and 1949. In the following decades the annual number of criminological publications on white-collar crime increases rapidly. The average annual numbers are, organized by five-year groups, 18 (1950–54), 28 (1955–59), 56 (1960–64), 86 (1965–69), 225 (1970–74), 379 (1975–79); the number of publications listed decreases again during the first half of the 1980s, from 426 (1979) to 312 (1980), 233 (1981), 276 (1982), 178 (1983), to 141 (1984—the last year included in the bibliography). More detailed analyses are needed to identify if this trend is also characteristic for country-specific bibliographies. A decrease in the number of American publications during the early 1980s would in fact be surprising given the sizable research funding program of the federal government during the Carter administration.

Centralized Efforts Against White-Collar Crime? Executive Branch, Legislative Branch, and Regulatory Agencies

The Justice System Improvement Act of 1979, the enabling legislation of the National Institute of Justice, included a special focus on white-collar crime and public corruption (Underwood 1982). The movement against white-collar crime, decentralized as its origins may have been, thus finally resulted in some centralized responses. The funding program corresponded well with President Carter's populist agenda and with his campaign promises to set an end to illegitimate and immoral practices of the powerful (Saxon 1980, pp. 89–92). Furthermore, this new initiative did not just include research funding but also new administrative and legislative strategies of the federal government.

The movement against offenses of the powerful was thus not exclusively decentralized. In fact, evidence suggests that the grass roots movement was closely interwoven with centralized responses of the federal government, which, however, were often ambivalent and frequently more symbolic in nature than a real threat to powerful offenders.

Executive Branch

Centralized efforts against white-collar crime by the executive branch can already be found during the 1970s when the U.S. Department of Justice and the FBI announced and implemented first steps against white-collar offenders. In the late 1970s, for example, the FBI reordered its enforcement policies, listing white-collar crime among its top investigative priorities; it considerably increased the proportion of resources devoted to white-collar investigations (including investigators) to 24 percent of its budget. In addition, the number of white-collar crime convictions resulting from FBI investigations rose from 292 (in 1973) to 3300 (in 1979), and, finally, the U.S. Justice Department underwent considerable restructuring during the second half of the 1970s, aimed at better investigations and prosecutions of powerful offenders (Simon and Swart 1984). Further, the Justice Department supported local experimental programs to fight economic crime through specialized units. By 1979, 62 such projects were active throughout the country, initiated by the National District Attorneys Association and funded by the Law Enforcement Assistance Agency (see, e.g., Whitcomb et al. 1979 on the Connecticut Economic Crime Unit).

Despite these trends, questions have been raised with regard to the seriousness and effectiveness of the new agenda. Still, in 1977, members of the Subcommittee on Civil and Constitutional Rights of the House Judiciary Committee, according to James Q. Wilson, made the criticism that the government, and especially the FBI, was "soft on establishment crime [and that the] FBI's idea of white-collar crime was welfare cheating and other examples of individual and, presumably, small-scale fraud against the government" (Wilson 1980, p. 9; quoted after Simon and Swart 1984, p. 108). This sentiment persisted among some members of the House for many years to come as the earlier citation of Representative and Chair of the Subcommittee on Criminal Justice John Conyers from Detroit demonstrates (U.S. House of Representatives, Subcommittee on Criminal Justice 1988, p. 490; see p. 2 of this volume). Pointing at several weak spots in the government's agenda, Simon and Swart (1984) cast doubt concerning the increasingly investigative and prosecutorial efforts against white-collar crime. Their first argument relates closely to the definitional issue expressed by Conyers.

> What is clear is that the Justice Department has drastically altered and expanded the usual definition of white-collar crime. . . . In 1976 the annual report of the FBI included under the rubric of white-collar crime "fraud, embezzlement, bribery, antitrust, perjury, conflict of interest, and related offenses." . . . In 1977, the definition was expanded to include "fraudulent practices in federal housing funds, veterans' benefits, and health education and welfare programs." . . . And in 1978, "government fraud, bank fraud, and embezzlement, and copyright violations" [according to the Senate Committee on Appropriations]. (Simon and Swart 1984, p. 109 and note 2)

Part of the increased resources devoted to white-collar crime investigations and prosecutions and part of the statistical gains in the fight against white-collar crime thus simply reflect more expansive definitions rather than greater success and true shifts in policy. And, more important, no information in the Attorney General's report on white-collar crime reveals the size of corporate firms or the level of corporate management involved in the Department's white-collar investigations.

> There are no reliable data at this time that would allow us to make a definite judgement regarding the socioeconomic status of the individuals, or the size of the corporate entities involved, in the FBI-Justice Department's white-collar crime investigations and prosecutions. (Simon and Swart 1984, p. 111)

One additional minor observation may further indicate the actual weight of white-collar crime concerns within the culture of the FBI. Simon and Swart (1984, p. 111) find that, among the 63 to 173 articles published annually in the FBI Law Enforcement Bulletin, from zero to a maximum of three deal with questions of white-collar crime.

In sum, while it is obvious that the executive branch of the federal government did respond to the increasing public concern with crimes of the powerful, it is uncertain how many white-collar cases were actually added to the Department's record. Much of the response appears to have been merely symbolic, an attempt to reestablish the legitimacy of the justice system, rather than a true effort to investigate and prosecute white-collar cases. It is also uncertain how many of the new "white-collar" cases actually concerned powerful actors in government and the economy against whom the public mistrust had been directed. There is reason to believe that much of the white-collar initiative simply expanded punitive responses to members of the lower middle and middle classes.

Finally, while the number of investigations and subsequent prosecution against powerful offenders did increase, the outcome may not be quite that dramatic for the target group. Many of the state's cases are successfully defeated already in the early stages of the criminal justice process. Mann's detailed study on *Defending White-Collar Crime* demonstrates that defense attorneys in high-level white-collar cases successfully use "managerial information control" as a fundamental defense strategy, typically long before charges have even be filed (Mann 1985, p. 8). As a result, most white-collar cases against powerful offenders are lost in the early phases of the criminal justice process.

Legislative Branch

It would be insufficient to judge government efforts against white-collar crime solely based on the record of the executive branch. Legislative steps need to be considered. While we have to concentrate on the federal level, we should mention that the famous Ford Pinto prosecution cited above would not have been possible if the state of Indiana had not passed a "reckless homicide act" just a few months before the fatal accident that initiated the prosecution (Cullen et al. 1987, p. 148).

In this context we concentrate on the more crucial federal legislative initiatives against white-collar crime. Here too the 1970s witnessed centralized initiatives, for example (Saxon 1980, pp. 24–30):

- During the 94th Congress, the Antitrust Procedures and Penalties Act of 1974 raised violations of the Sherman Antitrust Act from misdemeanors to felonies; the Antitrust Parens Patriae Act gave greater civil investigative power to the Justice Department's Antitrust Division and required corporations to announce significant mergers; and a provision in the 1976 Crime Control Act provided grants for the states to improve their antitrust enforcement capacities.
- During the 95th Congress, the Foreign Corrupt Practices Act prohibited bribery of foreign officials by any domestic concern; and PL 95-142 increased penalties in cases of fraud against Medicare and Medicaid programs.
- During the 96th Congress, the Federal Computer Systems Protection Act was passed, as well as the Justice System Improvement Act, which established the National Institute of Justice and mandated research funds for "efforts to detect, investigate, prosecute, and otherwise combat and prevent white-collar crime and public corruption" (cited after Saxon 1980, p. 27).

While this is not the place to provide a complete list of federal legislation against white-collar crime, more recent policy changes with regard to the sentencing of organizational offenders deserve special mention. Initiatives to develop more efficient alternatives are not new. Already in 1971 the National Commission on Reform of Federal Criminal Laws (Brown Commission) suggested to the U.S. Congress "several novel alternatives [in] the organizational sentencing debate: publicity, notice to victims, and probation" (Lofquist 1993, p. 159). The commission, however, did not provide any suggestions with regard to the implementation of such guidelines. Congress made use of the Brown Commission's report when it considered criminal code reform during the 1970s and early 1980s, until it passed the Sentencing Reform Act in 1984. This legislation demanded that fines and probation be used when the offender is an organization, and designated the newly created U.S. Sentencing Commission to specify the penalties (Lofquist 1993, p. 160). In 1991 the Commission submitted its final organizational sentencing guidelines to Congress. In them the Commission made organizational probation universally available and provided for "rehabilitative interventions." William Lofquist (1993) summarizes:

The court shall order a term of probation
—if necessary to secure satisfaction of other sanctions;
—if an organization of fifty or more employees lacks an effective program to prevent and detect law violations;
—if the organization or high level personnel participating in the offense have been convicted of a similar offense in the past five years;
—if necessary to ensure that changes are made within the organization to reduce the likelihood of future criminal conduct;
—if the sentence does not include a fine; or
—if necessary to accomplish one of the four purposes of sentencing (Lofquist 1993, p. 162).

Mandatory and discretionary conditions of organizational probation include:

—commission of no further crime (mandatory);
—payment of a fine or restitution, or performance of community service [mandatory; and optional:]
—publicity paid for by the defendant in media specified by the court detailing the crime, conviction, sentence, and remedial steps taken;
—development by the defendant, with court approval, of an effective program to prevent and detect future law violations;
—notification of employees and shareholders . . . ;
—periodic reports to the court . . . ; and
—periodic examinations of facilities and records, and interviews with employees by the court or a special probation officer to monitor compliance. (Lofquist 1993, p. 162)

While the success of implementing these new types of organizational
penalties is still uncertain, Lofquist is confident for several reasons: the
frequency with which probation is mandatory, the detailed conditions
of implementation of sentences, the nonadversarial nature of regulatory relations, and the fact that "the boundaries of corporate criminal
liability have increased substantially in the past two decades" (Lofquist
1993, p. 168).

This confidence is shared by Amitai Etzioni (1993, p. 156), who
analyzes the political process from which these organizational guidelines emerged. Etzioni describes the commission's withdrawal from
initial retribution and deterrence oriented guidelines which had been
based on severe fines. The withdrawal followed forceful opposition by
powerful economic lobbying groups, including the National Association of Manufacturers and the American Corporate Counsel Association. Liberal groups had not been involved in the debates to counter
the lobbying weight of business. Giving in to considerable political
pressure, the commission developed a new proposal which turned out
to be radically different from the first draft, in some instances reduc-
ing penalties by as much as 97 percent (Etzioni 1993, p. 150). The
new guidelines also faced opposition. While liberal groups made cautious attempts toward tougher standards, business groups attempted
to eliminate the idea of mandatory sentencing guidelines completely in
favor of voluntary policy statements. A letter in support of the guidelines written by former Deputy Attorney General Donald Ayer was
withdrawn "shortly after a meeting between members of the Business
Roundtable and White House Counsel C. Boyden Gray [and a subse-
quent] 'inquiry' from the White House to the Justice Department"
(Etzioni 1993, pp. 150–151).

The final organizational guidelines, proposed by the Commission in
its report from May 1, 1991, provided for penalties that are somewhat
enhanced beyond the previous lenient version. These guidelines also
included mitigating factors that would allow for easy reductions of the
"remaining penalties to small amounts, if not zero" (Etzioni 1993,
p. 151). In developing these mitigating factors, however, "the commission stumbled onto a rather important concept" (Etzioni 1993, p. 151)
when it included as one mitigating factor the installment of the internal
plans and compliance programs summarized above that would reduce
the likelihood of future offenses.

In sum, the interaction between the commission's punitive agenda
and the political pressure of economic lobbying groups and a conservative political climate resulted in the unexpected and initially
unplanned adoption of a concept of corporate self-regulation that, according to Braithwaite's in-depth study of the pharmaceutical indus-

try, is the most effective strategy against corporate crime (Braithwaite 1984, pp. 290–383). While this case illustrates the power of economic lobbying groups in defeating stern punitive measures in criminal justice policy making, it also demonstrates that potentially successful crime-fighting strategies may emerge despite industry resistance.

A Note on Regulatory Agencies

Important as responses of criminal justice agencies against white-collar and organizational crime may be, American criminal law continues to be the smaller force in this field when compared to administrative government regulation and sanctions. Clinard et al. (1979, p. XX) find that 85 percent of all sanctions against corporations are administrative in nature. Some of the more impressive recent American studies on the social context of industry regulation and the sanctioning of organizational and white-collar offenses have been done in the area of administrative law and regulatory agencies. Examples from the regulation of securities and savings and loan industries are especially instructive in this context.

In an in-depth study Susan Shapiro (1984) investigated the workings of the Securities and Exchange Commission (SEC). The function of the SEC is the protection of American capital markets. If companies want to offer securities for public sale, federal securities legislation first requires them to register with the SEC and to disclose and continuously update basic business and financial information. The SEC then serves as an informant to investors. It also regulates broker-dealers, investment advisors and companies, and stock exchanges. The agency's staff are responsible for enforcing the federal securities laws and conducting inspections, and finally investigating and instituting civil and administrative proceedings. Shapiro analyzed more than 500 of the agency's investigations, conducted between 1948 and 1972. One of her findings is of particular interest:

The typical scenes of wayward capitalism portrayed limited, undramatic securities frauds, enacted by small numbers of co-offenders, representing small, young, often fledgling corporations, taking in relatively few, often gullible investors. . . . In the typical case, offending organizations were neither prominent nor were they drawn from industries we might have expected. (Shapiro 1984, p. 42)

We do not know, of course, to what degree the pattern found by Shapiro reflects either the actual distribution of offenses or the agency's selection bias. The SEC, like all control agencies, may tend to investigate less complex cases with less powerful offenders rather than com-

plex cases against powerful organizations. To the degree to which this
is the case, Shapiro's finding would be consistent with findings or
suggestions of other studies cited above. It would further be similar to
the result of our case study of German white-collar crime legislation,
according to which control efforts, initially directed at the powerful,
may eventually be used to control the lower echelons of the white-
collar classes.

More drastic biases in the area of security regulation, however, seem
to result from interaction effects between regulatory action and responses by powerful investors. Research by Nancy Reichman (1991) on
events surrounding the 1987 stock market crash identifies such bias.
Reichman argues that security regulations tend to serve those investors
whose capacity to manage risk on their own is limited. Yet government
regulation competes with other, privatized forms of risk assessment.
"Players with greater capacity for risk management (e.g., access to
market intelligence, sizable reserves to cushion losses and enhanced
technologies for risk assessment) seek out new arrangements for man-
aging risk" (Reichman 1991, p. 263). Reichman demonstrates that
these innovations eventually undermine the regulatory program for
smaller scale investors who most depend on it. In a different sector of
regulation, Yeager comes to similar conclusions in his research on the
Environmental Protection Agency:

The results suggest that ostensibly neutral legal structures necessarily tend to
favor more powerful businesses and to burden smaller companies dispropor-
tionately. Smaller firms appear more frequently on lists of violators, indicating
that regulatory law reflects and reproduces systemic inequalities. (Yeager 1987,
p. 330; see also Yeager 1991)

A final example for the limits of regulatory action relates to the
savings and loan crisis of the 1980s, which has recently directed intense
public and scholarly attention at crimes committed within the savings
and loan industry (e.g., Calavita and Pontell 1990 and 1992, Pontell
and Calavita 1993). Three types of offenses have been identified as
typical for this industry: unlawful risk-taking, collective embezzlement,
and covering up (Calavita and Pontell 1990, pp. 316–328). These
offenses have, it seems, at least partly been encouraged by government
action. Calavita and Pontell (1990, p. 328) cite the House Committee
on Government Operations that identified " 'serious deficiencies' in the
way the federal banking regulators and the Justice Department have
handled fraud in the banking and thrift industry."

In general, the offenses result in part from three sets of factors
related to regulation. First, the size of the examination staff of the

Federal Home Loan Bank Board (FHLBB), the primary regulatory agency, was almost stable between 1966 and 1986 despite the manyfold increase of workload (Calavita and Pontell 1990, p. 330). Second, networks of influence also seem to have played a major role in the failed regulation. Among them is the crucial role played by the U.S. League of Savings Associations, a powerful lobbying group of thrift executives, in the nomination of the head of the FHLBB. The link between the industry and the regulatory agency is even closer since members of the Board are typically drawn from the industry itself. In addition, networks of interest connect members of Congress with representatives of the thrift industry (Calavita and Pontell 1990, pp. 331, 332). Third, regulation faces major structural impediments. Calavita and Pontell (1990, p. 335) point to "finance capitalism in the United States [as] a 'casino' economy," characterized by profit taking from often highly speculative investments, as the most important structural dilemma.

In this context, the role of the state is not to establish optimal conditions for productive activity, as it was in industrial capitalism, but to shore up the illusion and minimize the potential for panic. Thus it makes sense that the same deregulators who dismantled all restrictions on the savings and loan industry in the name of the free market deviated so dramatically from their own conviction and *increased* deposit insurance. The contradiction underlying the thrift debacle, then, is that the casino economy is based on illusion but that illusion must be preserved at all costs. (Calavita and Pontell 1990, p. 338)

While the structural implications of finance capitalism for government regulation and the network configurations between government and banking industry warrant further systematic research, the evidence provided by Calavita and Pontell suggests two conclusions. First, the interaction effect among communication networks connecting government and financial markets, the power potentials of this industry, and the sensitive nature of the financial markets imply considerable dilemmas for regulatory agencies as well as criminal law enforcement.

Furthermore, the writings of Calavita and Pontell confirm the general public impression that the potential for criminal offenses in this industry under conditions of deregulation during the 1980s was considerable and probably resulted in rapid increases in criminal behavior. Further research should investigate if this conclusion can be generalized to other economic sectors that experienced deregulation during the same decade. If it can be generalized, then the increasing visibility of white-collar cases in the criminal justice system during the 1980s may not reflect enhanced enforcement efforts but simply the vastly growing number of white-collar offenses during this period.

Conclusions: Commonalities, Divergences, and Theory

Three types of questions are raised by this brief and selective overview of the diverse American literature on the control and punishment of powerful offenders. First, does the American experience confirm the theoretical conclusions drawn for the German case study? Second, what factors may account for some amazing cross-national similarities in the patterns of white-collar crime control? And third, what other factors might explain the considerable country-specific particularities which we have also found? In concluding we briefly address each of these questions separately for the movement and the centralized response.

The Movement Against White-Collar Crime: Structural Conditions and the Impact of Group Action on Outcomes

Was the movement against white-collar crime driven by structural conditions and functional demands or by specific social actors and conflict groups? There is no doubt that structural factors played an important role. It appears that the end of the cold war and of the external threat constituted a condition that provided new opportunities to express mistrust toward the elite of one's own country. This would confirm, for a specific case, a more general social regularity long described in the sociology of conflict (Coser 1956; Simmel 1955).

In addition, changes in economic structures lend themselves to criticism against the country's leadership. For example, the redistribution of economic power between industrialized countries and oil-producing countries from the Third World, most visible during the 1973 oil embargo, highlighted the power limits of industrialized countries. Furthermore, limits to the potential for unlimited economic growth had become visible and were made public with the famous report to the Club of Rome (Meadows et al. 1972). It became apparent that the national leadership could not be blindly trusted and that the old recipes it advocated might no longer work.

Structural conditions for American industry had already changed before the 1973 "oil shock." The industries of war-torn Europe and Japan had gained new strength in the 1950s and appeared as competitors on world and American markets during the 1960s. Cullen et al. (1986) show that the hasty and careless design of certain American car models during the late 1960s and early 1970s was at least partly a response to increasing competitive pressure by foreign producers of small cars.

Historical "accidents," such as Watergate and the Three Mile Island nuclear accident in the United States, helped amplify the perception of new dilemmas and challenges. The fact that the movements against the powerful and white-collar offenders appeared at the same time in many countries, however, cautions us from concentrating too much on factors that were specific to the United States.

While the structural conditions cited provided fertile ground for new challenges to political and economic elites, specific social actors and conflict groups were needed to translate structural conflicts into actual challenges of established elites. Conflict groups need to be considered for two reasons. First, the quality of the particular conflict groups involved has implications for the nature, the functions, and the consequences of the challenge. And second, which groups get involved in the challenge depends on the particular nature of the structural conflict in each society and on the country-specific institutionalization of interest groups.

Why did certain groups get involved in the challenge in the two countries under consideration? Individual moral entrepreneurs played visible roles in both societies. Most outstanding in America was consumer advocate Ralph Nader. Nader gained wide publicity and was heard in Congressional hearings on several legislative initiatives. Individual moral entrepreneurs played visible roles in Germany as well. The writer Günther Walraff, for example, sought incognito employment in steel plants, shipbuilding yards, and banking corporations, and conducted incognito interviews with Catholic bishops, politicians, and other holders of power. He published his widely read observations in the tradition of the American muckrakers from the early part of the century (Walraff 1970 and 1985; one of the authors [JJS] read Walraff's writings in 1971 as part of his German high school curriculum). Yet activists in Germany do not get access to official functions as easily as in the United States. While they reflect public opinion (at least that of progressive groups) and reinforce this opinion through their writings, they do not get formal access to the political sector, for example through legislative hearings, as their American counterparts do. This difference in the role of activist moral entrepreneurs is a reflection of the highly integrated and neo-corporate structure of interest representation in Germany, which contrasts with the much more fluid and fragmented structure of public interest representation in America (Skocpol 1985). On a more speculative note, the greater public visibility of activist moral entrepreneurs in the United States might result in a steadier reminder to the public that the issues have not disappeared and in more continuous public support for the cause.

It is not surprising that the one German moral entrepreneur who did play a major role in the preparation of legislative drafts was the jurisprudent Klaus Tiedemann. He made his way through the institutionalized channels of the German Lawyers Association when this association declared economic crime its primary criminal law theme for its 1972 meetings. Around the same time, Tiedemann had also been asked by the (then newly Social Democratic) Federal Department of Justice to write an expert opinion on economic crime.

In general, lawyers seem to have played a crucial role in claims making against powerful offenders in both countries. In Germany during the late 1960s, several innovations in the fight against economic crime were initiated by local and state level law enforcement agencies. These initiatives, while singular events, preceded the action taken by the Lawyers Association almost simultaneously with the Federal Department of Justice. The latter force soon resulted in a centralized response, the creation of the commission for the fight against economic crime (Chapter 4) and the subsequent legislative process. Prosecutors played a crucial and, it seems, much more pronounced role within the American legal profession than their German counterparts. Further decentralization and movement characterize their role, as illustrated by Katz (1980).

The different roles played by lawyers can best be explained if we consider differences between the roles of prosecutors in the two countries. In addition to the particular career opportunities connected with the white-collar issue for American prosecutors (Katz 1980) and the individual rights and equality concerns of the American legal tradition (Cullen et al. 1987) two differences stand out. First, the political quality of the prosecutor's role in the United States, expressed most clearly by elections and political appointments to the office and the subsequent political careers of many officeholders, contrasts with the life tenured professional career model of prosecutors in the German system. American prosecutors have, therefore, much more reason to anticipate and follow public sentiment than their German counterparts. Second, prosecutors in the United States are not only compelled to anticipate and follow public sentiment, they also have the *discretion* to do so, in contrast to German prosecutors who are bound by the legality principle and obliged to charge all cases where criminal behavior is indicated (on modifications see Chapter 5 and Stemmler 1993). German prosecutors were thus prominent in the debate of the Lawyers Association Meeting and in the Justice Department's Commission attempting to put the law on the books. The German legal profession is more closely interwoven with the state than the American profession, thus reflecting the more neo-corporate character of public life in that country (Rueschemeyer 1973, Halliday 1989).

Just as with moral entrepreneurs, initiatives by German lawyers were absorbed by and channeled through centralized government action. The nation-specific features of the legal profession and the role of prosecutors had consequences for the way in which they got involved in the process. As in the case of activists and moral entrepreneurs, the different quality of their involvement influenced the outcome. While the German response to white-collar crime was probably more strategically planned and centrally directed, as opposed to the predominant "case motif" of the American response, it was also thoroughly exposed to the mediating lobbying effects of powerful actors from the economic sector in the neo-corporate setting of German legislative action.

The Centralized Response: Structure, Conflict Groups, and Institutional Theory

Can a functionalist approach explain the trends in American control efforts against organizational and white-collar actors? Some of the conclusions drawn in the previous section apply here as well. There seems to be little doubt that structural and functional demands play an important role. Coleman (1982) has demonstrated that the number of corporate actors has grown rapidly throughout this century. An increasing number of transactions are performed by corporate actors and corporate actors find increasing public attention, for example in news media reporting. It should thus not be surprising that a society that uses penal law to discipline its members will extend this law to corporate actors as well. In addition, new functional needs demand responses in the United States just as in Germany, as the recent legal regulation of computer-related behavior illustrates. Furthermore, many functionalist analyses have demonstrated that modern states introduce control administrations to compensate for the negative side effects of market capitalism (Sweezy 1942; Therborn 1978), a situation that was especially characteristic for the American New Deal. Others have shown that such intervention, while possibly fulfilling its regulatory functions, also politicizes areas of action that libertarian ideology has assigned to markets (Habermas 1975; Wright 1978). These authors have further argued that government, in order to respond to the resulting legitimatory challenges, uses "technocratization" (Stryker 1989, 1990a, 1990b), the introduction of technocratic expertise into regulatory decision making. The proposed function of this strategy is not simply more rational goal achievement through expert knowledge, but the renewed depoliticization of government intervention. This strategy too faces limits, as Stryker (1990b) has demonstrated in her profound analyses on the workings of the National Labor Relations Board and the Social Security Board.

While this brief summary of a very complex debate illustrates the concern of state action with functional demands, it also illustrates the limits and confusions surrounding conflicting functional requirements of state action, especially with regard to the achievement of policy purposes versus legitimatory constraints. The American case illustrates additional problems of functionalist analysis. For example, actors' concrete network ties may prove to be decisive for the outcome of regulatory action in America just as in the German bid rigging case— even though the outcome may be highly damaging to the general economy. The failures of the savings and loan regulations as analyzed by Calavita and Pontell (1990) are but one example. Another illustration for the crucial importance of network ties and communication patterns is provided by Cullen et al. (1987, pp. 155–159) when they present excerpts from conversations between President Nixon and leaders of the American automobile industry. Again, articulated interests of economic actors may well be in conflict with long-term functional needs of the economy and yet nonetheless prevail.

What about the Marxist versus pluralist debate? While the movement against powerful offenders was certainly carried by pluralist forces, the American case confirms the German experience that different social forces, more specifically powerful groups, are superior in the legislative and legal processes. The power of business has been impressively demonstrated, for example, in the setting of sentencing guidelines (Etzioni 1993) and in the savings and loan case (Calavita and Pontell 1990). These forces often turn the control impetus not against members of the working classes, but against smaller firms and lower ranks of the white-collar class, as the studies by Reichman (1991) and Yeager (1987, 1991) have shown for administrative control, and Katz (1980) and Simon and Swart (1984) have indicated for criminal law enforcement. Such outcomes point to conflict within social classes and thus challenge a purely class-oriented analysis.

Furthermore, representatives of different state control agencies with various organization-specific interests were highly represented in the law-making process in both the United States and Germany. In the American case their interests are also not in accordance with those of industry and frequently not in harmony with each other. Instead, each organization attempts to extend its resources and control capacities and to maintain its legitimacy. A rich body of literature, representing the institutional approach to organizational analysis, has recently demonstrated that the behavior of modern organizations is often driven more by legitimatory needs than by concerns with functional efficacy (DiMaggio and Powell 1983; Edelman 1990; Hagan, Hewitt, and Alwin 1979; Meyer and Rowan 1977; Sutton 1988, pp. 232–258). Our analysis has indicated also that much of enforcement agencies' action serves symbolic and legitimatory purposes, aiming to reestablish the credibility of the law and that of particular control agencies. The analysis of Cullen et al. (1987) has demonstrated this motivation for government action in the Ford Pinto case. They use the term revitalization movement to describe legal initiatives against powerful offenders. But they argue that such action was limited to a few highly visible cases. This is confirmed by Katz's (1980) analysis of the prosecutorial movement and Simon and Swart's (1984) study on the white-collar policies of the FBI. These agency actions managed simultaneously to achieve three purposes: to satisfy movements against the powerful, to avoid disturbing the holders of important power positions, and to secure and expand their own control bureaucracies.

Despite the basic and partly astounding American-German similarities in the public response to crimes of the powerful, there is one difference that we would like to explore briefly. While it is difficult to quantify the degree of intervention for a precise comparison, it appears as though critical public sentiment and debate on the behavior of the powerful is not just older but also more persistent in the United States than in Germany. It further seems that government action in seasons of public mistrust has also been somewhat more forceful in the United States than in Germany—despite all the limitations discussed above. We have pointed to some comparative American-German particularities that may explain this difference. We finally summarize these differences and hint at some more that future research should consider.[2]

First, group and class conflicts are more intense and are carried out more openly in the United States than in Germany. When mistrust increases against one social category, for example corporate executives, we thus expect this mistrust to be more intense and more visible than in Germany.

Second, and closely related, group conflicts in Germany are carried out through large, inclusive, neo-corporate interest organizations. This situation allows less access for social activists (such as the consumer advocate Ralph Nader in the United States) to the German political process. Further the institutionalization of grassroots, special interest, and local movements in the United States allows such activists to keep issues in the public limelight for extensive periods of time.

2. Savelsberg (1994) discusses several of these American-German differences in greater detail with regard to divergent trends in criminal punishment.

Third, the legal profession is more independent from government in the United States than in Germany. While the German legal profession is closely affiliated with the state (Rueschemeyer 1973; Halliday 1987), its American counterpart is relatively autonomous. For example, access to the bar is controlled by state examinations in the former and bar examinations in the latter. Individual rights, as reflected in the U.S. Constitution, are more strongly rooted in American than in German jurisprudence. The same holds for the notion of individual responsibility. It thus makes some sense when Cullen et al. (1987, p. 18) interpret parts of the American movement against powerful offenders as a revitalization movement of the American legal profession. They suggest that the profession felt threatened by increasing doubts about the idea of equality before the law. In Germany, on the other hand, lawyers are much more involved in purposive government action, a situation which more easily overshadows concerns with formally equal rights of individuals than in the United States.

Another American-German difference is of interest in this context. Given the closer affiliation of the German legal profession with the state, it may not be that surprising that much of the German fight against white-collar offenders was directed against the economic sector, while the American attack was directed against members of the political sector as well.

Fourth, private and highly competitive media markets in the United States suggest that public sentiments are reflected in sensational news about issues that reflect public concerns, such as white-collar crime. While we found such a reflection in Germany as well, for example from the private press, major portions of German media (until recently all television and radio programming) are governed by neo-corporate boards that include all major interest organizations of the country, unions, employer associations, political parties, and major religious organizations. While we do not have comparable media analyses, we expect more responsiveness to public concerns in the American than in the German media, including concerns with white-collar crime.

Fifth, public sentiment is more intensely mirrored by regular public opinion polling in the United States than in Germany. This factor is likely to serve as a positive feedback loop and to further add to trends in public sentiments.

Sixth, decision makers in the American government system are likely to be more responsive to public outcries than their German counterparts. Roth (1987) contrasts the U.S. political system of increasing universalistic personalism with the universalistic bureaucracies in the FRG. Universalistic personalism in the American legislative system means that representatives and senators are relatively independent from their political parties but personally accountable to their constituency. They are greatly and immediately dependent on their constituency whenever an issue is highly politicized. Representatives in the FRG are more oriented toward party platforms and faction discipline and relatively independent from public opinion. Their nomination depends on intra-party decisions and their election depends on party membership since voters, in practice, vote for a candidate as the member of a political party rather than for an individual with a particular voting record.

In the executive branch as well, political actors in the United States are more closely related to the public and to different sectors of society. At the same time they are often less firmly integrated in the political system than their German colleagues. The administrative leadership is more strongly exposed to public opinion given the popular presidential vote (as opposed to parliamentary elections of chancellors in the FRG). It is no surprise then that President Jimmy Carter, elected on a populist agenda in the aftermath of Watergate, attempted to move the white-collar issue ahead.

U.S.-German differences in the judicial branch resemble those in the legislative branch. While most judges and prosecutors in the United States are either elected or nominated and confirmed in political processes, those in the FRG are appointed as civil servants with tenured positions, early in their professional career, and usually according to academic achievement tests. They are more firmly embedded in the political-administrative system than their American counterparts (Rueschemeyer 1973; Halliday 1989). They do not depend on public approval and are therefore more independent from public opinion.

All of this suggests more active political and legal responses to claims making against white-collar crime in the United States than in Germany. Some of the U.S. activism may in fact spill over to other countries as happened in the case of computer offenses. Members of the German Justice Department traveled to Washington in 1985. Their purpose was to learn about new U.S. computer crime legislation before they extended their set of computer provisions in the final bill of the Second Law. It is important to note in this context that two countries, such as the United States and Germany, are rarely fully independent units of analysis. They may be influenced by a same third source, for example international events or, more specifically, changes in international law. Or one country, most likely the larger and more powerful one, may influence the other, as the above example indicates. Spillover may also be the result of conquest. After the end of World War II, for example, U.S. antitrust law was imposed on Germany during the postwar occupation. A few years after the end of this occupation, however, the German government changed antitrust law back from criminal statutes to purely administrative law.

Finally, the difference between U.S. and German responses to claims making obviously reflects different patterns. Vogel (1986), in his comparison of U.S. and British environmental policy calls these patterns "national styles of regulation," contrasting mostly adversarial, litigious, and rule-bound regulation in the United States with mostly cooperative, consensual, and discretionary regulation in Britain. Hawkins (1984) provides supporting evidence for the British case in his study of water pollution control. Kelman (1981) identifies similarly different styles of regulation in his Swedish-U.S. comparison of regulatory policy. Numerous studies on German regulatory policy in a diversity of areas, such as environmental, industrial, and welfare regulation, have demonstrated that the style of German regulation is much more comparable to the British and Swedish cases and thus in contrast to the U.S. case (Mayntz 1980 and 1983; Wollmann 1980).

In conclusion, the general style of regulation and government control, much more characterized by neo-corporatist mechanisms in many European countries including Germany, may partially explain why the German response to claims making against the powerful appears to have been less active and confrontational than the U.S. response. But, perhaps more important, parliamentarians, civil servants, and criminal justice lawyers in the United States are much more exposed to shifts of public knowledge, ideology, and resulting political pressure than their German counterparts, who base their decisions on bureaucratically produced knowledge. The same amount of public upset about crimes of the powerful is thus likely to lead to more intense rhetorical responses and more political and legal action in the United States. It should also be noted that the United States surpassed the late Soviet Union and South Africa during the 1980s to become the world's leader in criminal punishment. This reflects the strongly punitive strategies of this decade, and it is likely that some of this trend spilled over to the higher social classes. Finally, it is quite possible that the white-collar offense rate increased faster in America during the 1980s than in other western countries. The savings and loan case is an example that this may have been one consequence of deregulation in several industries during this decade. Again, we would expect more attention to white-collar cases in the U.S. situation.

Whether political and legal activism in the United States results in a better protection of the public, consumers, and lower classes in this country than in Germany is a separate question which we cannot answer here. Some of the literature discussed in this section suggests doubts.

References

DOCUMENTS

Numerous government documents and media sources referred to in this book are sufficiently referenced in the text so that a bibliographical identification of the sources is possible on that basis. For reasons of practicability these sources are not again included in the following reference list. Documents from lobby groups are also precisely referenced in the text. Copies of these documents are filed by the researchers. They are, however, not accessible for public use for reasons of confidentiality.

SCHOLARLY LITERATURE

Adler, Jeffrey S. 1989. "A Historical Analysis of the Law of Vagrancy." *Criminology* 27:209–229.
Akers, Ronald L. 1975. "The Professional Association and the Legal Regulation of Practice." Pp. 80–92 in *Law and Control in Society*, edited by Ronald L. Akers and Richard Hawkins. Englewood Cliffs, N.J.: Prentice Hall.
Alber, Jens. 1982. *Vom Armenhaus zum Wohlfahrtsstaat: Analysen zur Entwicklung der Sozialversicherung in Westeuropa*. Frankfurt: Campus.
Arzt, Gunther. 1976. *Der Ruf nach Recht und Ordnung: Ursachen und Folgen der Kriminalitätsfurcht in den USA und in Deutschland*. Tübingen: J. C. B. Mohr.
Aubert, Vilhelm. 1952. "White-Collar Crime and Social Structure." *American Journal of Sociology* 63:263–271.
Axelrod, Robert M. 1976. "The Cognitive Mapping Approach to Decision Making." Pp. 3–17 in *Structure of Decision: The Cognitive Map of Political Elites*, edited by Robert M. Axelrod. Princeton, N.J.: Princeton University Press.
Allensbacher Berichte. 1983. No. 27. Allensbach: Institut für Demoskopie.
Bachrach, Peter and Morton S. Baratz. 1970. *Power and Poverty: Theory and Practice*. New York: Oxford University Press.
Becker, Howard S. 1973. *Outsiders: Studies in the Sociology of Deviance*. New York: Free Press.
Benson, Michael and Esteban Walker. 1988. "Sentencing the White Collar Offender." *American Sociological Review* 53:294–302.
Berckhauer, Friedrich Helmut. 1980. "Die Strafverfolgung bei Wirtschaftsdelikten in der Bundesrepublik Deutschland." Pp. 218–241 in *Empirische*

Kriminologie, edited by Forschungsgruppe Kriminologie. Freiburg/Breisgau: Max-Planck-Institut für ausländisches und internationales Strafrecht.

Berckhauer, Friedhelm and Joachim J. Savelsberg. 1987. "Vom Aufbruch zur Resignation: Die 'Bundesweite Erfassung' wurde in aller Stille zu Grabe getragen." *Kriminalistik* 41:242–246.

Black, Donald. 1976. *The Behavior of Law*. Orlando, Flor.: Academic Press.

———. 1987. "Compensation and the Social Structure of Misfortune." *Law and Society Review* 21:563–584.

Blankenburg, Erhard and Hubert Treiber. 1975. "Der politische Prozeß der Definition von kriminellem Verhalten." *Kriminologisches Journal* 4:252–262.

Bonham, Matthew and Martin Shapiro. 1984. Personal communication.

Braithwaite, John. 1984. *Corporate Crime in the Pharmaceutical Industry*. London: Routledge and Kegan Paul.

Breuer, Stefan. 1977. "Politik und Recht in Prozeß der Rationalisierung." *Leviathan* 5:53–100.

Bundesminister der Justiz, ed. 1980. *Bekämpfung der Wirtschaftskriminalität*. Bonn: Bundesministerium der Justiz.

Bussman, Kai-D. 1991. *Die Entdeckung der Informalität: Über Aushandlungen im Strafverfahren und ihre juristische Konstruktion*. Badan-Baden: Nomos.

Bussmann, Kai-D. and Christian Lüdemann. 1992. *Klassenjustiz oder Verfahrensökonomie? Über Aushandlungen im Strafverfahren*. Pfaffenweiler: Centaurus.

Bustos, Ramírez, J. M. Scriva, R. Bergalli, A. deSola, M. T. Miralles, and M. Peats. 1982. "Genese und Legitimation von strafrechtlichen Normen in Spanien am Beispiel der Umweltkriminalität." *Kriminologisches Journal* 14:213–24.

Calavita, Kitty and Henry N. Pontell. 1990. "'Heads I Win, Tails You Lose': Deregulation, Crime, and Crisis in the Savings and Loan Industry." *Crime and Delinquency* 36:309–341.

Carson, Wesley G. 1974. "The Sociology of Crime and the Emergence of Criminal Laws." Pp. 67–90 in *Deviance and Social Control*, edited by Paul Rock and Mary McIntosh. London: Tavistock Publications.

Chambliss, William J. 1964. "Sociological Analysis of the Law of Vagrancy." *Social Problems*: 12:67–77.

———. 1989. "On Trashing Marxist Criminology." *Criminology* 27:231–250.

Chambliss, William J. and Robert B. Seidman. 1982. *Law, Order, and Power*. Reading, Mass.: Addison-Wesley.

Clinard, Marshall B., Peter Yeager, Jeanne Brissette, David Petrashek, and Elizabeth Harries. 1979. *Illegal Corporate Behavior*. Washington, D.C.: U.S. Department of Justice.

Coffee, John C. 1981. "'No soul to damn, no body to kick': An Unscandalized Inquiry into the Problem of Corporate Punishment." *Michigan Law Review* 79:386–459.

Coleman, James S. 1982. *The Asymmetric Society*. Syracuse, N.Y.: Syracuse University Press.

Coleman, James William. 1987. "Toward an Integrated Theory of White-Collar Crime." *American Journal of Sociology* 93:406–439.

Coser, Lewis A. 1956. *The Functions of Social Conflict*. Glencoe, Ill.: Free Press.

Crenson, Matthew A. 1971. *The Un-Politics of Air Pollution: A Study of Non-Decisionmaking in the Cities*. Baltimore: Johns Hopkins University Press.

Cullen, Francis T., William J. Maakestad, and Gray Cavender. 1987. *Cor-

porate Crime Under Attack: The Ford Pinto Case and Beyond. Cincinnati, Oh.: Anderson.

Dahrendorf, Ralf. 1974. "Die Funktionen sozialer Konflikte." Pp. 263–77 in *Pfade aus Utopia* by Ralf Dahrendorf. München: Piper.

Dencker, Friedrich and R. Hamm. 1988. *Der Vergleich im Strafprozeß.* Hamburg: Metzner.

Deutsch, Karl W. 1971. "Macht und Kommunikation in der internationalen Gesellschaft." Pp. 471–483 in *Theorie des Sozialen Wandels*, edited by Wolfgang Zapf. Köln: Kiepenheuer.

Deutscher Bundestag. 1963. *Protokoll der 70. Plenarsitzung am 28. März 1963* [Minutes of the 70th Plenary Session]. Bonn: Deutscher Bundestag.

———. 1986. *Beschlußempfehlung und Bericht des Rechtsausschusses* (Drucksache 10/5058) Bonn: Deutscher Bundestag.

DiMaggio, Paul and Walter Powell. 1983. "The Iron Cage Revisited: Institutional Ismorphism and Collective Rationality in Organizational Fields." *American Sociological Review* 48:147–160.

Doig, Jameson W., Douglas E. Phillips, and Tycho Manson. 1984. "Deterring Illegal Behavior by Officials of Complex Organizations." *Criminal Justice Ethics* 3:27–56.

Durkheim, Émile. 1893. *De la division du travail social.* Paris: Dissertation, published 1930 by Presses Universitaires de France.

———. 1899/1900. "Deux lois de l'évolution pénale." *Année Sociologique* 4:65–95.

Edelhertz, Herbert and Thomas D. Overcast, eds. 1982. *White-Collar Crime: An Agenda for Research.* Lexington, Mass.: Lexington Books.

Edelman, Lauren B. 1990. "Legal Environments and Organizational Governance: The Expansion of Due Process in the American Workplace." *American Journal of Sociology* 95:1401–40.

Eder, Klaus. 1978. "Zur Rationalisierungsproblematik des modernen Rechts." *Soziale Welt* 29:247–256.

Etzioni, Amitai. 1968. *The Active Society: A Theory of Societal and Political Processes.* New York: Free Press.

———. 1993. "The U.S. Sentencing Commission on Corporate Crime: A Critique." Pp. 147–156 in *White-Collar Crime: Offenses in Business, Politics, and the Professions*, edited by Gilbert Geis and Paul Jesilow. Annals of the American Academy of Political and Social Science, vol. 525. Newbury Park, Calif.: Sage Publications.

Fisse, Brent and John Braithwaite. 1983. *The Impact of Publicity on Corporate Offenders.* Albany: State University of New York Press.

Fisse, Brent and Peter A. French, eds. 1985. *Corrigible Corporations and Unruly Law.* San Antonio, Tex.: Trinity University Press.

Gallhofer, Irmtraud N. and Willem E. Saris. 1984. "Explanation of the Use of Decision Rules: A Study of Foreign Policy Decisions." Amsterdam: Research Unit for Decision Behavior and Sociometry, University of Amsterdam.

Geis, Gilbert. 1985. "Criminological Perspectives on Corporate Regulation: A Review of Recent Research." Pp. 63–84 in *Corrigible Corporations and Unruly Law*, edited by Brent Fisse and Peter A. French. San Antonio, Tex.: Trinity University Press.

———. 1992. "The Heavy Electrical Equipment Antitrust Cases of 1961." Pp. 74–94 in *Corporate and Governmental Deviance: Problems of Organizational*

Behavior in Contemporary Society (4th edition), edited by M. David Ermann and Richard J. Lundman. New York: Oxford University Press.

Geis, Gilbert and Ezra Stotland, eds. 1980. *White-Collar Crime: Theory and Research*. Beverly Hills, Calif.: Sage Publications.

Gessner, Volkmar. 1984. "Rechtssoziologie und Rechtspraxis. Zur Rezeption von empirischer Rechtsforschung." Pp. 69–112 in *Empirische Rechtsforschung zwischen Wissenschaft und Politik: Zur Problemlage rechtssoziologischer Auftragsforschung*, edited by K. Plett and K. Ziegert. Tübingen: Mohr/Siebeck.

Gillin, Todd. 1980. *The Whole World is Watching: Media in the Making and Unmaking of the New Left*. Berkeley: University of California Press.

Gusfield, Joseph R. 1967. "Moral Passage: The Symbolic Process in Public Designations of Deviance." *Social Problems* 14:175–188.

Habermas, Jürgen. 1975. *Legitimation Crisis*. Boston: Beacon Press.

Haferkamp, Hans. 1980. *Herrschaft und Strafrecht: Theorien der Normentstehung und Strafrechtsetzung*. Opladen: Westdeutscher Verlag.

———. 1983. *Soziologie der Herrschaft*. Opladen: Westdeutscher Verlag.

———. 1984. "Herrschaftsverlust und Sanktionsverzicht: Kritische Bemerkungen zur Theorie des starken Staates, der neuen sozialen Kontrolle und des ideellen Abolitionismus." *Kriminologisches Journal* 16:112–31.

———. 1990. "Leistungsangleichung und Individualisierung: Unbegriffene Ursachen der Kriminalität und des Strafens in modernen Wohlfahrtsstaaten." Pp. 7–62 in *Wohlfahrtsstaat und seine Politik des Strafens*, edited by H. Haferkamp. Opladen: Westdeutscher Verlag.

Hagan, John. 1980. "The Legislation of Crime and Delinquency: A Review of Theory, Method, and Research." *Law and Society Review* 14:603–628.

Hagan, John, John D. Hewitt, and Duane F. Alwin. 1979. "Ceremonial Justice: Crime and Punishment in a Loosely Coupled System." *Social Forces* 58:506–529.

Hagan, John, Ilene H. Nagel, and Celesta Albonetti. 1980. "The Differential Sentencing of White-Collar Offenders in Ten Federal District Courts." *American Sociological Review* 45:802–820.

Hagan, John and Patricia Parker. 1985. "White-Collar Crime and Punishment." *American Sociological Review* 50:302–316.

Hall, Jerome. 1952. *Theft, Law, and Society*. Indianapolis: Bobbs-Merrill.

Halliday, Terence C. 1987. *Beyond Monopoly: Lawyers, State Crises, and Professional Empowerment*. Chicago: University of Chicago Press.

———. 1989. "Legal Professions and Politics: Neocorporatist Variations on the Pluralist Theme of Liberal Democracies." Pp. 375–426 in *Lawyers in Society: Comparative Theories*, edited by Richard L. Abel and Philip S. C. Lewis. Berkeley: University of California Press.

Hawkins, Keith. 1984. *Environment and Enforcement: Regulation and the Social Definition of Pollution*. Oxford: Clarendon Press.

Heiland, Hans-Günther and Christian Lüdemann. 1992. "Machtdifferentiale in Konfigurationen einfacher und höherer Komplexität: ein Anwendung der Machttheorie von Norbert Elias auf Aushandlungen in Strafverfahren." *Kölner Zeitschrift für Soziologie und Sozialpsychologie* 44:35–54.

Hempel, Carl G. 1958. "The Theoretician's Dilemma: A Study in the Logic of Theory Construction." Pp. 37–98 in *Concepts, Theories, and the Mind-Body Problem*, edited by Herbert Feigl and Michael Scriven. Minnesota Studies in the Philosophy of Science vol. 2. Minneapolis: University of Minnesota Press.

Hippel, Rudolf von. 1898. "Beiträge zur Geschichte der Freiheitsstrafe." *Zeitschrift für die gesamten Strafrechtswissenschaften* 18:419–494 and 608–662.

Hopkins, Andrew. 1975. "On the Sociology of Criminal Law." *Social Problems* 22:608–619.

Kaiser, Günther. 1980. *Kriminologie.* Heidelberg: Müller.

Kaiser, Günther and Volker Meinberg. 1984. "'Tuschelverfahren' und 'Millionärsparagraph'?" *Neue Zeitschrift für Strafrecht* 4:343–350.

Kalberg, Stephen. 1987. "West German and American Interaction Forms: One Level of Structured Misunderstanding." *Theory, Culture, and Society* 4:603–618.

———. 1992. "Culture and the Locus of Work in Contemporary West Germany: a Weberian Configurational Analysis." Pp. 324–65 in *Theory of Culture*, edited by Neil J. Smelser and Richard Münch. Berkeley: University of California Press.

Kassebaum, Gene G. and David A. Ward. 1991. "Analysis, Reanalysis, and Meta Analysis of Correctional Treatment Effectiveness: Is the Question What Works or Who Works?" *Sociological Practice Review* 2:159–168.

Katz, Jack. 1980. "The Social Movement against White-Collar Crime." Pp. 161–184 in *Criminology Review Yearbook.* Volume 2, edited by Egon Bittner and Sheldon Messinger. Beverly Hills, Calif.: Sage Publications.

Kelman, Steven. 1981. *Regulating America, Regulating Sweden: A Comparative Study of Occupational Safety and Health Policy.* Cambridge, Mass.: MIT Press.

Lautmann, Rüdiger. 1975. "Einige Thesen zum Zusammenhang von Kriminalisierung und Legitimation." University of Bremen (unpublished manuscript).

Liebl, Karlhans. 1984. *Die Bundesweite Erfassung von Wirtschaftsstraftaten nach einheitlichen Gesichtspunkten: Ergebnisse und Analysen für die Jahre 1974 bis 1981.* Freiburg/Breisgau: Max Planck-Institut für Internationales und Vergleichendes Strafrecht.

Liebl, Hildegard and Karlhans Liebl. 1985. *International Bibliography of Economic Crime.* Pfaffenweiler: Centaurus.

Lipset, Seymour Martin and William Schneider. 1983. *The Confidence Gap: Business, Labor, and Government in the Public Mind.* New York: Free Press.

Lofquist, William S. 1993. "Organizational Probation and the U.S. Sentencing Commission." Pp. 157–169 in *White-Collar Crime*, edited by Gilbert Geis and Paul Jesilow. Annals of the American Academy of Political and Social Science, Vol. 525. Newbury Park, Calif.: Sage Publications.

Lüdemann, Christian and Kai-D. Bussmann. 1989. "Diversionschancen der Mächtigen? Eine empirische Studie über Absprachen im Strafprozeß." *Kriminologisches Journal* 21:54–72.

Malinowski, Bronislaw. 1926. *Crime and Custom in Savage Society.* London: Routledge and Kegan Paul.

Mann, Kenneth. 1985. *Defending White-Collar Crime: A Portrait of Attorneys at Work.* New Haven, Conn.: Yale University Press.

Mann, Kenneth, Stanton Wheeler, and Austin Sarat. 1980. "Sentencing the White-Collar Offender." *American Criminal Law Review* 17:479–500.

Matthes, Joachim. 1964. *Gesellschaftspolitische Konzeptionen im Sozialhilferecht: Zur soziologischen Kritik der neuen deutschen Sozialhilfegesetzgebung 1961.* Stuttgart: Enke.

Mayntz, Renate. 1983. "Implementation regulativer Politik." Pp. 50–74 in

Implementation politischer Programme II: Ansätze zur Theoriebildung, edited by Renate Mayntz. Opladen: Westdeutscher Verlag.

————, ed. 1980. *Implementation politischer Programme: empirische Forschungsberichte*. Königstein: Athenäum.

————, ed. 1983. *Implementation politischer Programme II: Ansätze zur Theoriebildung*. Opladen: Westdeutscher Verlag.

Meadows, Donella H., Dennis L. Meadows, Jorgen Randers, and William W. Behrens III. 1972. *The Limits to Growth: A Report for the Club of Rome's Project on the Predicament of Mankind*. New York: Universe Books.

Meyer, John W., and Brian Rowan. 1977. "Institutionalized Organizations: Formal Structure as Myth and Ceremony." *American Journal of Sociology* 83:340–363.

Möhrenschlager, Manfred. 1984. "Die Reform des deutschen Wirtschaftsstrafrechts: Seine kriminologischen und kriminalpolitischen Grundlagen." Pp. 227–241 in *Politische Kriminalität und Wirtschaftskriminalität*. Diessenhofen: Rüegger.

Pilgram, Arno and Heinz Steinert. 1975. "Ansätze zur politisch-ökonomischen Analyse der Strafrechtsreform in Österreich." *Kriminologisches Journal* 7:263–77.

Popitz, Heinrich. 1968. *Prozesse der Machtbildung*. Tübingen: Mohr.

Pohoryles, Ronald. 1981. "Determinanten und Resultate der österreichischen Strafrechtsreform in den siebziger Jahren." *Österreichische Zeitschrift für Politikwissenschaft* 10:39–50.

Pontell Henry N. and Kitty Calavita. 1993. "White-Collar Crime and the Savings and Loan Scandal." Pp. 31–45 in *White-Collar Crime*, edited by Gilbert Geis and Paul Jesilow. Annals of the American Academy of Political and Social Science, Vol. 525. Newbury Park, Calif.: Sage Publications.

Quinney, Richard. 1975. "Crime Control in Capitalist Society: A Critical Philosophy of Legal Order." Pp. 181–202 in *Critical Criminology*, edited by Ian Taylor, Paul Walton, and Jock Young. London: Routledge and Kegan Paul.

Radcliffe-Brown, A. R. 1935. "On the Concept of Function in Social Science." *American Anthropologist* 37:395–96.

Redeker, Konrad. 1978. "Juristentag mit Licht und Schatten." *Zeitschrift für Rechtspolitik* 10:225–28.

Reichman, Nancy. 1991. "Regulating Risky Business: Dilemmas in Security Regulation." *Law and Policy* 13:263–295.

Roby, Pamela A. 1975. "Politics and Criminal Law: Revision of the New York State Penal Law on Prostitution." Pp. 93–108 in *Law and Control in Society*, edited by Ronald L. Akers and Richard Hawkins. Englewood Cliffs, N.J.: Prentice-Hall.

Ross, Edward A. 1907. *Sin and Society*. Boston: Houghton Mifflin.

Roth, Günther. 1987. *Politische Herrschaft und Persönliche Freiheit: Heidelberger Max Weber-Vorlesungen 1983*. Frankfurt: Suhrkamp.

Rueschemeyer, Dietrich. 1973. *Lawyers and their Society*. Cambridge: Harvard University Press.

Rusche, Georg and Otto Kirchheimer. 1939. *Social Structure and Punishment*. New York: Columbia University Press.

Sack, Fritz. 1983. "Rechtsfriede und sozialer Friede." *Bewährungshilfe* 15:7.

Saris, Willem and Irmtraud N. Gallhofer. 1982. "A Coding Procedure for Empirical Research on Decision Making." University of Amsterdam (unpublished manuscript).

Savelsberg, Joachim J. 1980. *Kommunale Autonomie: Autonomie, Macht und Entscheidungen in Gemeinden*. Frankfurt: Haag und Herchen.

———. 1987a. "The Making of Criminal Law Norms in Welfare States: Economic Crime in West Germany." *Law and Society Review* 21:529–61.

———. 1987b. "Von der Genese zur Implementation von Wirtschaftsstrafrecht: Klassen-, schicht- und sektorspezifische Aushandlungsprozesse?" *Kriminologisches Journal* 19:193–211.

———. 1988. "Rationalities and Experts in the Making of Criminal Law Against Economic Crime." *Law and Policy* 10: 215–252.

———. 1992. "Law That Does Not Fit Society: Sentencing Guidelines as a Neoclassical Reaction to the Dilemmas of Substantivized Law." *American Journal of Sociology* 97:1346–1381.

———. 1994. "Knowledge, Domination, and Criminal Punishment." *American Journal of Sociology* 99 (January).

Savelsberg, Joachim J. and Peter Brühl. 1988. *Politik und Wirtschaftsstrafrecht*. Leverkusen: Leske und Budrich.

Saxon, Miriam S. 1980. "White-Collar Crime: The Problem and the Federal Response." Report No. 80–84 EPU, Congressional Research Service (unpublished).

Schick, Peter J. 1981. "Kritische Überlegungen zur Genese des Straftatbestandes." Pp. 84–99 in *Gesetzgebungslehre*, edited by G. Winkler and B. Schilcher. Wien/New York.

Schluchter, Wolfgang. 1981. *The Rise of Western Rationalism: Max Weber's Developmental History*. Berkeley: University of California Press.

Schneider, Joseph W. 1985. "Social Problems: The Constructionist View." *Annual Review of Sociology* 11:209–229.

Schöch, Heinz. 1984. "Strafverfolgung und Strafzumessung bei Steuerhinterzihung." Pp. 227–241 in *Politische Kriminalität und Wirtschaftskriminalität*, edited by Walter T. Haesler. Diessenhofen: Rüegger.

Schoreit, Arnim. 1974. "Kriminalpolitik und Rationalität." *Juristenzeitung* 29:254–257.

Schubarth, Martin. 1980. "Das Verhältnis von Strafrechtswissenschaft und Gesetzgebung im Wirtschaftsstrafrecht." *Zeitschrift für die gesamte Strafrechtswissenschaft* 92:80–106.

Schumann, Karl F. 1974. "Gegenstand und Erkenntnisinteressen einer konflikttheoretischen Kriminologie." Pp. 69–84 in *Kritische Kriminologie*, edited by Arbeitskreis Junger Kriminologen. München: Juventa.

Schünemann, Bernd. 1989. "Die Verständigung im Strafprozeß: Wunderwaffe oder Bankrotterklärung der Verteidigung?" *Neue Jurische Wochenschrift* 42:1895–1903.

Skocpol, Theda. 1985. "Bringing the State Back in: Strategies of Analysis in Current Research." Pp. 3–43 in *Bringing the State Back In*, edited by Peter B. Evans, Dietrich Rueschemeyer, and Theda Skocpol. Cambridge: Cambridge University Press.

Seidel, Horst. 1980. "Prozesse der Normsetzung. Inhaltsanalyse parlamentarischer Beratungen der Strafrechtsreform in der Bundesrepublik Deutschland." Universität Bremen: Unpublished Paper.

Shapiro, Susan P. 1984. *Wayward Capitalists: Target of the Securities and Exchange Commission*. New Haven, Conn.: Yale University Press.

Shrager, Laura Shill and James F. Short. 1980. "How Serious a Crime? Perceptions of Organizational and Common Crimes." Pp. 14–31 in *White-Collar*

Crime: Theory and Research, edited by Gilbert Geis and Ezra Stotland. Beverly Hills, Calif.: Sage Publications.

Simmel, Georg. 1955. "Conflict." Pp. 11–123 in Simmel, *Conflict and the Web of Group Affiliations*, translated by Kurt H. Wolff and Reinhard Bendix. New York: Free Press.

Simon, David R. and Stanley L. Swart. 1984. "The Justice Department Focuses on White-Collar Crime: Promises and Pitfalls." *Crime and Delinquency* 30:107–119.

Stangl, Wolfgang. 1985. *Die neue Gerechtigkeit: Strafrechtsreform in Östrreich 1954–1975*. Wien: Verlag für Gesellschaftskritik.

Steinert, Heinz. 1978. "On the Functions of Criminal Law." *Contemporary Crises* 2:167–93.

Stemmler, Susanne. 1993. "German Plea Bargaining: How It Actually Works." Paper presented at the Annual Meetings of the Law and Society Association, Chicago.

Stryker, Robin. 1989. "Limits on Technocratization of Law." *American Sociological Review* 54:341–358.

———. 1990a. "A Tale of Two Agencies: Class, Political-Institutional, and Organizational Factors Affecting State Reliance on Social Science." *Politics and Society* 18:101–141.

———. 1990b. "Science, Class, and the Welfare State: A Class-Centered Functional Approach." *American Journal of Sociology* 96:684–726.

Sutherland, Edwin H. 1940. "White Collar Criminality." *American Sociological Review* 5:1–12.

———. 1945. "Is 'White Collar Crime' Crime?" *American Sociological Review* 10:132–39.

———. 1949. *White Collar Crime*. New York: Holt, Rinehart, and Winston.

Sutton, John R. 1988. *Stubborn Children: Controlling Delinquency in the United States, 1640–1981*. Berkeley: University of California Press.

Sweezy, Paul M. 1942. *The Theory of Capitalist Development*. New York: Monthly Review Press.

Therborn, Goran. 1978. *What Does the Ruling Class Do When it Rules?* London: New Left Books.

Tiedemann, Klaus. 1976. *Wirtschaftsstrafrecht und Wirtschaftskriminalität*. Reinbek: Rowohlt.

Trubek, David M. 1972. "Max Weber on Law and the Rise of Capitalism." *Wisconsin Law Review* 1972/3:720–753.

———. 1985. "Reconstructing Max Weber's Sociology of Law." *Stanford Law Review* 37:919–936.

———. 1986. "Max Weber's Tragic Modernism and the Study of Law in Society." *Law and Society Review* 20:573–598.

Turk, Austin. 1976. "Law as a Weapon in Social Conflict." *Social Problems* 23:276–291.

Turkel, Gerald. 1980. "Rational Law and Boundary Maintenance: Legitimating the 1971 Lockheed Loan Guarantee." *Law and Society Review* 15:41–77.

Turner, Bryan S. 1981. *For Weber: Essays on the Sociology of Fate*. Boston: Routledge and Kegan Paul.

Underwood, James L. 1982. National Institute of Justice Program on White-Collar Crime (National Institute of Justice memorandum to Stanley E. Morris, Associate Attorney General, unpublished).

U.S. House of Representatives, Subcommittee on Criminal Justice. 1988. *Hear-*

ings on the Sentencing Guidelines. Washington, D.C.: U.S. Government Printing Office.

Vogel, David. 1986. *National Styles of Regulation: Environmental Policy in Great Britain and the United States.* Ithaca, N.Y.: Cornell University Press.

Walraff, Günther. 1970. *Industriereportagen: Als Arbeiter in deutschen Großbetrieben.* Hamburg: Rowohlt.

———. 1985. *Ganz Unten.* Köln: Kiepenheuer und Witsch.

Waldmann, Peter. 1979. "Zur Genese von Strafrechtsnormen." *Kriminologisches Journal* 11:102–23.

Weber, Max. [1976]. *Wirtschaft und Gesellschaft.* Tübingen: J. C. B. Mohr; reprint, 1947 Mohr/Siebeck.

———. [1978]. *Economy and Society.* Berkeley: University of California Press.

Weisburd, David, Stanton Wheeler, Elin Waring, and Nancy Bode. 1991. *Crimes of the Middle Classes: White-Collar Offenders in the Federal Courts.* New Haven, Conn.: Yale University Press.

Wheeler, Stanton and Mitchell L. Rothman. 1982. "The Organization as a Weapon in White-Collar Crime." *Michigan Law Review* 80:1406–26.

Wheeler, Stanton, David Weisburd, and Nancy Bode. 1982. "Sentencing the White-Collar Offender: Rhetoric and Reality." *American Sociological Review* 47:641–659.

Whitcomb, Debra, Louis Frisina, and Robert L. Spangenberg. 1979. *An Exemplary Project: Connecticut Economic Crime Unit.* Washington, D.C.: U.S. Government Printing Office.

Wilson, James Q. 1980. "The Changing FBI: The Road to Abscam." *The Public Interest* 62:3–14.

Winckelmann, Johannes. 1976. *Erläuterungsband zu Max Weber: Wirtschaft und Gesellschaft.* Tübingen: Mohr/Siebeck.

Wollmann, Hellmut, ed. 1980. *Politik im Dickicht der Bürokratie: Beiträge zur Implementationsforschung.* Opladen: Westdeutscher Verlag.

Wright, Eric Olin. 1978. *Class, Crisis, and the State.* London: New Left Books.

Yeager, Peter C. 1987. "Structural Bias in Regulatory Law Enforcement: The Case of the U.S. Environmental Protection Agency." *Social Problems* 34:330–344.

———. 1991. *The Limits of Law: The Public Regulation of Private Pollution.* New York: Cambridge University Press.

Index

commission, 85–86; influence on legislative drafting, 7, 93–103, 138; United States, 150–51
Lockheed Aircraft, 23
Lofquist, William, 149, 150
Lüdemann, Christian, 118

McCarthy, Joseph R., 141
Malinowski, Bronislaw, 19
Mann, Kenneth, 118, 148
Marxism, xii, 13, 14, 23, 133, 158
Marxist functionalism, 13, 20, 21, 132
Max Planck Institute, Freiburg, 34, 118
Methodology, xii–xiii, 21, 27–30
Mill, John Stuart, 136
Mining industry, 22
"Moral entrepreneurs," 27, 142, 146, 155–56
"Moral functionalism," 19–20
"Moral Marxism," 19, 20

Nader, Ralph, 144, 155, 159
"Naive action theory," 26
National Association of Manufacturers (U.S.), 150
National Commission on Reform of Federal Criminal Laws (U.S., Brown Commission), 149–50
National District Attorneys Association (U.S.), 146
National Highway Traffic Safety Administration (U.S.), 145
National Institute of Justice (U.S.), 145, 148
New Deal, 141, 157
"New little masters," 17–18, 23, 24
News media: claims making by, xi, 33, 36–39, 57, 142; policy demands, 45; selection bias in, 46; U.S.-German comparison, 142, 160
Nixon, Richard M., 143, 158
Noll, Peter, 47–48, 49, 50–51

Oil embargo (1973), 89, 154

Parafisci (semi-governmental organizations), 40
Particularization of law, 15, 23–24, 107, 134
Pilgram, Arno, 20

Pluralist (differentiation) theory, xii, 13, 14–19, 131, 158
Pohoryles, Ronald, 136
Police, 45, 60
Political decision making, 26, 33, 53, 104, 136
Political exchange value, 39–40
Political parties, 4; and cognitive maps, 126; policy demands, 43; and political exchange value, 39–40; and power accumulation, 88–89; U.S.-German comparison, 160–61
Political process, 7–8, 26, 87, 88, 138, 139
Political sector, 60, 87, 124, 137, 138, 155, 160
Political systems, 23, 87–88, 104
Politicians, 29–30, 89, 132, 160–61
Politicization, 27
Pontell, Henry N., 152, 153, 158
Power, 22; communication and, 13–14, 24–26, 137–38; and domination, 17, 18, 25; potentials, 23, 138; and rationalities, 23–24; structures, 20
Price fixing, criminalization of: cognitive maps and, 76, 107, 109, 111, 113; expert commission and, 70; industry lobbying against, 22, 132, 133; labor unions and, 22, 133
Privatization, 23
Probation, 149, 150
"Problem graph," 72
Prosecution, 35–36
Prosecutors: in expert commission, 60; policy demands, 45; in U.S. efforts against white-collar crime, 143, 145–46; U.S.-German comparison, 156, 157, 161
Public opinion, 36, 46, 142, 160, 161
Public sector, 23
Purposive rationality, 53–54, 76, 78, 123

Quinney, Richard, 137

Radcliffe-Brown, A. R., 19
Rationalism, 14–15
Rationalities, 13–14, 19, 22, 26, 53–54
Regulatory agencies, 151–53
Reichman, Nancy, 152, 158
Research, 48, 49
Roosevelt, Franklin D., 141
Ross, Edward, 140

University of Pennsylvania Press
Law in Social Context Series

Roy B. Fleming, Peter F. Nardulli, and James Eisenstein. *The Craft of Justice: Politics and Work in Criminal Court Communities.* 1992
Joel F. Handler. *Law and the Search for Community.* 1990
Robert M. Hayden. *Social Courts in Theory and Practice: Yugoslav Workers' Courts in Comparative Perspective.* 1991
Sheila Jasanoff, editor. *Learning from Disaster: Risk Management After Bhopal.* 1994
Richard Lempert and Joseph Sanders. *An Invitation to Law and Social Science.* 1989
Candace McCoy. *The Politics of Plea Bargaining: California's Proposition 8 and Its Impact.* 1992
Joseph Rees. *Reforming the Workplace: A Study of Self-Regulation in Occupational Safety.* 1988
Jeffrey A. Roth, John T. Scholz, and Ann Dryden Witte, editors. *Taxpayer Compliance. Volume I: An Agenda for Research.* 1989
Jeffrey A. Roth, John T. Scholz, and Ann Dryden Witte, editors. *Taxpayer Compliance. Volume II: Social Science Perspectives.* 1989